Joseph Butler

Human Nature and Other Sermons

Joseph Butler

Human Nature and Other Sermons

ISBN/EAN: 9783744742139

Printed in Europe, USA, Canada, Australia, Japan

Cover: Foto ©Lupo / pixelio.de

More available books at **www.hansebooks.com**

CASSELL'S NATIONAL LIBRARY.

HUMAN NATURE

AND

OTHER SERMONS

BY

JOSEPH BUTLER,

BISHOP OF DURHAM.

CASSELL & COMPANY, Limited:
LONDON, PARIS, NEW YORK & MELBOURNE.
1887.

INTRODUCTION.

JOSEPH BUTLER was born in 1692, youngest of eight children of a linendraper at Wantage, in Berkshire. His father was a Presbyterian, and after education at the Wantage Free Grammar School Joseph Butler was sent to be educated for the Presbyterian ministry in a training academy at Gloucester, which was afterwards removed to Tewkesbury. There he had a friend and comrade, Secker, who afterwards became Archbishop of Canterbury. Butler and Secker inquired actively, and there was foreshadowing of his future in the fact that in 1713, at the age of twenty-one, Butler was engaged in anonymous discussion with Samuel Clarke upon his book on the *à priori* demonstration of the Divine Existence and Attributes.

When the time drew near for call to the ministry, Butler, like his friend Secker, had reasoned himself into accordance with the teaching of the Church of England. Butler's father did not oppose his strong desire to enter the Church, and he was entered in 1714 at Oriel College, Oxford. At college a strong friendship was established between Butler and a fellow-student, Edward Talbot, whose father was a Bishop, formerly of Oxford and Salisbury, then of Durham.

Through Talbot's influence Butler obtained in 1718 the office of Preacher in the Rolls Chapel, which he held for the next eight years. In 1722 Talbot died, and on his death-bed urged his father on behalf of his friend Butler. The Bishop accordingly presented Joseph Butler to the living of Houghton-le-Spring. But it was found that costs of dilapidations were beyond his means at Houghton, and Butler had a dangerous regard for building works. He was preferred two years afterwards to the living of Stanhope, which then became vacant, and which yielded a substantial income. Butler sought nothing for himself, his simplicity of character, real worth, and rare intellectual power, secured him friends, and the love of two of them—Talbot first, and afterwards Secker, who made his own way in the Church, and became strong enough to put his friend as well as himself in the way of worldly advancement, secured for Butler all the patronage he had, until the Queen also became his active friend.

Joseph Butler was seven years at Stanhope, quietly devoted to his parish duties, preaching, studying, and writing his "Analogy of Religion, Natural and Revealed, to the Constitution and Course of Nature." In 1727, while still at Stanhope, he was appointed to a stall in Durham Cathedral. Secker, having become chaplain to the Queen, encouraged her in admiration of Butler's sermons. He told her that the author was not dead, but buried, and secured her active interest in his behalf. From Talbot, who had become Lord

Chancellor, Secker had no difficulty in obtaining for Butler a chaplaincy which exempted him from the necessity of residence at Stanhope. Butler, in accepting it, stipulated for permission to live and work in his parish for six months in every year. Next he was made chaplain to the King, and Rector of St. James's, upon which he gave up Stanhope. In 1736 Queen Caroline appointed him her Clerk of the Closet, an office which gave Butler the duty of attendance upon her for two hours every evening. In that year he published his "Analogy," of which the purpose was to meet, on its own ground, the scepticism of his day. The Queen died in 1737, and, in accordance with the strong desire expressed in her last days, in 1738 Butler was made a Bishop. But his Bishopric was Bristol, worth only £300 or £400 a year. The King added the Deanery of St. Paul's, when that became vacant in 1740, and in 1750, towards the close of his life, Joseph Butler was translated to the Bishopric of Durham. He died in 1752.

No man could be less self-seeking. He owed his rise in the Church wholly to the intellectual power and substantial worth of character that inspired strong friendship. Seeing how little he sought worldly advancement for himself, while others were pressing and scrambling, Butler's friends used their opportunities of winning for him the advancement he deserved. He was happiest in doing his work, of which a chief part was in his study, where he employed his philosophic mind in strengthening the foundations of religious faith. Faith in God was attacked by men who claimed especially to be philosophers, and they were best met by the man who had, beyond all other divines of his day—some might not be afraid to add, of any day—the philosophic mind.

H. M.

HUMAN NATURE,

AND OTHER SERMONS.

SERMON I.

UPON HUMAN NATURE.

ROMANS xii. 4, 5.

For as we have many members in one body, and all members have not the same office: so we, being many, are one body in Christ, and every one members one of another.

THE Epistles in the New Testament have all of them a particular reference to the condition and usages of the Christian world at the time they were written. Therefore as they cannot be thoroughly understood unless that condition and those usages are known and attended to, so, further, though they be known, yet if they be discontinued or changed, exhortations, precepts, and illustrations of things, which refer to such circumstances now ceased or altered, cannot at this time be urged in that manner and with that force which they were to the primitive Christians. Thus the text now before us, in its first intent and design, relates to the decent management of those extraordinary gifts which were then in the Church,* but which are now totally ceased. And even as to the allusion that "we are one body in Christ," though what the apostle here intends is equally true of Christians in all circumstances, and the consideration of it is plainly still an additional motive, over and above moral considerations, to the discharge of the several duties and offices of a Christian, yet it is manifest this allusion must have appeared with much greater force to those who, by the many difficulties they went through for the sake of their religion, were led to keep always in view the relation they stood in to their Saviour, who had undergone the same: to those, who, from the idolatries of all around them, and their ill-treatment, were taught to consider themselves as not of the world in which they lived, but as a distinct society of themselves; with laws and ends, and principles of life and action, quite contrary to those which the world professed themselves at that time influenced by. Hence the relation of a Christian was by them considered as nearer than that of affinity and blood; and they almost literally esteemed themselves as members one of another.

It cannot, indeed, possibly be denied, that our being God's creatures, and virtue being the natural law we are born under, and the whole constitution of man being plainly adapted to it, are prior obligations to piety and

* 1 Cor. xii

virtue than the consideration that God sent his Son into the world to save it, and the motives which arise from the peculiar relation of Christians as members one of another under Christ our head. However, though all this be allowed, as it expressly is by the inspired writers, yet it is manifest that Christians at the time of the Revelation, and immediately after, could not but insist mostly upon considerations of this latter kind.

These observations show the original particular reference to the text, and the peculiar force with which the thing intended by the allusion in it must have been felt by the primitive Christian world. They likewise afford a reason for treating it at this time in a more general way.

The relation which the several parts or members of the natural body have to each other and to the whole body is here compared to the relation which each particular person in society has to other particular persons and to the whole society; and the latter is intended to be illustrated by the former. And if there be a likeness between these two relations, the consequence is obvious: that the latter shows us we were intended to do good to others, as the former shows us that the several members of the natural body were intended to be instruments of good to each other and to the whole body. But as there is scarce any ground for a comparison between society and the mere material body, this without the mind being a dead unactive thing, much less can the comparison be carried to any length. And since the apostle speaks of the several members as having distinct offices, which implies the mind, it cannot be thought an allowable liberty, instead of the *body* and *its members*, to substitute the *whole nature of man*, and *all the variety of internal principles which belong to it.* And then the comparison will be between the nature of man as respecting self, and tending to private good, his own preservation and happiness; and the nature of man as having respect to society, and tending to promote public good, the happiness of that society. These ends do indeed perfectly coincide; and to aim at public and private good are so far from being inconsistent that they mutually promote each other: yet in the following discourse they must be considered as entirely distinct; otherwise the nature of man as tending to one, or as tending to the other, cannot be compared. There can no comparison be made, without considering the things compared as distinct and different.

From this review and comparison of the nature of man as respecting self and as respecting society, it will plainly appear that *there are as real and the same kind of indications in human nature, that we were made for society and to do good to our fellow-creatures, as that we were intended to take care of our own life and health and private good: and that the same objections lie against one of these assertions as against the other.* For,

First, there is a natural principle of *benevolence* * in

---

* Suppose a man of learning to be writing a grave book upon *human nature*, and to show in several parts of it that he had an insight into the subject he was considering, amongst other things, the following one would require to be accounted for—the appearance of benevolence or good-will in men towards each other in the instances of natural relation, and in others.[1] Cautious of being deceived with outward show, he retires within himself to see exactly what that is in the mind of man from whence this appearance proceeds; and, upon deep reflection, asserts the principle in the mind to be only the love of power, and delight in the exercise of it. Would not everybody think here was a mistake of one word for another—that the philosopher was contemplating and accounting for some other *human actions*, some other behaviour of man to man? And could any one be thoroughly satisfied that what is commonly called benevolence or good-will was really the affection meant, but only by being made to understand that this learned person had a general hypothesis, to which the appearance of good-will could no otherwise be reconciled? That what has this appearance is often nothing but ambition; that delight in superiority often (suppose always) mixes itself with benevolence, only makes it more specious to call it ambition than hunger, of the two: but in reality that passion does no more account for the whole appearances of good-will than this appetite does. Is there not often the appearance of one man's wishing that good to another, which he knows himself unable to procure him; and rejoicing in it, though bestowed by a third person? And can love of power any way possibly come in to account for this desire or delight? Is there not often the appearance of men's distinguishing between two or more persons, preferring one before another, to do good to, in cases where love of power cannot in the least account for the distinction and preference? For this principle can no otherwise distinguish between objects than as it is a greater instance and exertion of power to do good to one rather than to another. Again, suppose good-will in the mind of man to be nothing but delight in the exercise of power: men might indeed be restrained by distant and accidental consideration; but these restraints being removed, they would have a disposition to, and delight in, mischief as an exercise and proof of power: and this disposition and delight would arise from, or

[1] Hobbes, "Of Human Nature," c. ix. § 7.

man, which is in some degree to *society* what *self-love* is to the *individual*. And if there be in mankind any disposition to friendship; if there be any such thing as be the same principle in the mind, as a disposition to and delight in charity. Thus cruelty, as distinct from envy and resentment, would be exactly the same in the mind of man as good-will: that one tends to the happiness, the other to the misery, of our fellow-creatures, is, it seems, merely an accidental circumstance, which the mind has not the least regard to. These are the absurdities which even men of capacity run into when they have occasion to belie their nature, and will perversely disclaim that image of God which was originally stamped upon it, the traces of which, however faint, are plainly discernible upon the mind of man.

If any person can in earnest doubt whether there be such a thing as good-will in one man towards another (for the question is not concerning either the degree or extensiveness of it, but concerning the affection itself), let it be observed that *whether man be thus, or otherwise constituted, what is the inward frame in this particular* is a mere question of fact or natural history, not provable immediately by reason. It is therefore to be judged of and determined in the same way other facts or matters of natural history are—by appealing to the external senses, or inward perceptions, respectively, as the matter under consideration is cognisable by one or the other: by arguing from acknowledged facts and actions; for a great number of actions in the same kind, in different circumstances, and respecting different objects, will prove to a certainty what principles they do not, and to the greatest probability what principles they do, proceed from: and, lastly, by the testimony of mankind. Now, that there is some degree of benevolence amongst men may be as strongly and plainly proved in all these ways, as it could possibly be proved, supposing there was this affection in our nature. And should any one think fit to assert that resentment in the mind of man was absolutely nothing but reasonable concern for our own safety, the falsity of this, and what is the real nature of that passion, could be shown in no other ways than those in which it may be shown that there is such a thing in *some degree* as *real* good-will in man towards man. It is sufficient that the seeds of it be implanted in our nature by God. There is, it is owned, much left for us to do upon our own heart and temper; to cultivate, to improve, to call it forth, to exercise it in a steady, uniform manner. This is our work: this is virtue and religion.

compassion—for compassion is momentary love—if there be any such thing as the paternal or filial affections; if there be any affection in human nature, the object and end of which is the good of another, this is itself benevolence, or the love of another. Be it ever so short, be it in ever so low a degree, or ever so unhappily confined, it proves the assertion, and points out what we were designed for, as really as though it were in a higher degree and more extensive. I must, however, remind you that though benevolence and self-love are different, though the former tends most directly to public good, and the latter to private, yet they are so perfectly coincident that the greatest satisfactions to ourselves depend upon our having benevolence in a due degree; and that self-love is one chief security of our right behaviour towards society. It may be added that their mutual coinciding, so that we can scarce promote one without the other, is equally a proof that we were made for both.

Secondly, this will further appear, from observing that the *several passions* and *affections*, which are distinct* both from benevolence and self-love, do in

---

* Everybody makes a distinction between self-love and the several particular passions, appetites, and affections; and yet they are often confounded again. That they are totally different, will be seen by any one who will distinguish between the passions and appetites *themselves*, and *endeavouring* after the means of their gratification. Consider the appetite of hunger, and the desire of esteem: these being the occasion both of pleasure and pain, the coolest *self-love*, as well as the appetites and passions themselves, may put us upon

general contribute and lead us to *public* good as really as to *private*. It might be thought too minute and particular, and would carry us too great a length, to distinguish between and compare together the several passions or appetites distinct from benevolence, whose primary use and intention is the security and good of society, and the passions distinct from self-love, whose primary intention and design is the security and good of the individual.* It is enough to the present

---

making use of the *proper methods of obtaining* that pleasure, and avoiding that pain; but the *feelings themselves*, the pain of hunger and shame, and the delight from esteem, are no more self-love than they are anything in the world. Though a man hated himself, he would as much feel the pain of hunger as he would that of the gout; and it is plainly supposable there may be creatures with self-love in them to the highest degree, who may be quite insensible and indifferent (as men in some cases are) to the contempt and esteem of those upon whom their happiness does not in some further respects depend. And as self-love and the several particular passions and appetites are in themselves totally different, so that some actions proceed from one and some from the other will be manifest to any who will observe the two following very supposable cases. One man rushes upon certain ruin for the gratification of a present desire: nobody will call the principle of this action self-love. Suppose another man to go through some laborious work upon promise of a great reward, without any distinct knowledge what the reward will be: this course of action cannot be ascribed to any particular passion. The former of these actions is plainly to be imputed to some particular passion or affection; the latter as plainly to the general affection or principle of self-love. That there are some particular pursuits or actions concerning which we cannot determine how far they are owing to one, and how far to the other, proceeds from this, that the two principles are frequently mixed together, and run up into each other. This distinction is further explained in the Eleventh Sermon.

* If any desire to see this distinction and comparison made in a particular instance, the appetite and passion now mentioned may

argument that desire of esteem from others, contempt and esteem of them, love of society as distinct from affection to the good of it, indignation against successful vice—that these are public affections or passions, have an immediate respect to others, naturally lead us to regulate our behaviour in such a manner as will be of service to our fellow-creatures. If any or all of these may be considered likewise as private affections, as tending to private good, this does not hinder them from being public affections too, or destroy the good influence of them upon society, and their tendency to public good. It may be added that as persons without any conviction from reason of the desirableness of life would yet of course preserve it merely from the appetite of hunger, so, by acting merely from regard (suppose) to reputation, without any consideration of the good of others, men often contribute to public good. In both these instances they are plainly instruments in the hands of another, in the hands of Providence, to carry on ends—the preservation

serve for one. Hunger is to be considered as a private appetite, because the end for which it was given us is the preservation of the individual. Desire of esteem is a public passion; because the end for which it was given us is to regulate our behaviour towards society. The respect which this has to private good is as remote as the respect that has to public good; and the appetite is no more self-love than the passion is benevolence. The object and end of the former is merely food; the object and end of the latter is merely esteem; but the latter can no more be gratified without contributing to the good of society, than the former can be gratified without contributing to the preservation of the individual.

of the individual and good of society—which they themselves have not in their view or intention. The sum is, men have various appetites, passions, and particular affections, quite distinct both from self-love and from benevolence: all of these have a tendency to promote both public and private good, and may be considered as respecting others and ourselves equally and in common; but some of them seem most immediately to respect others, or tend to public good; others of them most immediately to respect self, or tend to private good: as the former are not benevolence, so the latter are not self-love: neither sort are instances of our love either to ourselves or others, but only instances of our Maker's care and love both of the individual and the species, and proofs that He intended we should be instruments of good to each other, as well as that we should be so to ourselves.

Thirdly, there is a principle of reflection in men, by which they distinguish between, approve and disapprove their own actions. We are plainly constituted such sort of creatures as to reflect upon our own nature. The mind can take a view of what passes within itself, its propensions, aversions, passions, affections as respecting such objects, and in such degrees; and of the several actions consequent thereupon. In this survey it approves of one, disapproves of another, and towards a third is affected in neither of these ways, but is quite indifferent. This principle in man, by which he approves or disapproves his heart, temper, and actions, is conscience; for this is the strict sense of the word, though sometimes it is used so as to take in more. And that this faculty tends to restrain men from doing mischief to each other, and leads them to do good, is too manifest to need being insisted upon. Thus a parent has the affection of love to his children: this leads him to take care of, to educate, to make due provision for them—the natural affection leads to this: but the reflection that it is his proper business, what belongs to him, that it is right and commendable so to do—this, added to the affection, becomes a much more settled principle, and carries him on through more labour and difficulties for the sake of his children than he would undergo from that affection alone, if he thought it, and the cause of action it led to, either indifferent or criminal. This indeed is impossible, to do that which is good and not to approve of it; for which reason they are frequently not considered as distinct, though they really are: for men often approve of the actions of others which they will not imitate, and likewise do that which they approve not. It cannot possibly be denied that there is this principle of reflection or conscience in human nature. Suppose a man to relieve an innocent person in great distress; suppose the same man afterwards, in the fury of anger, to do the greatest mischief to a person who had given no just cause of offence. To aggravate the injury, add the circumstances of former friendship and obligation from the injured person; let the man who is supposed to have done these two different actions coolly reflect upon them afterwards, without regard to their consequences to himself: to assert that any common man would be affected in the same way towards these different actions, that he would make no distinction between them, but approve or disapprove them equally, is too glaring a falsity to need being confuted. There is therefore this principle of reflection or conscience in mankind. It is needless to compare the respect it has to private good with the respect it has to public; since it plainly tends as much to the latter as to the former, and is commonly thought to tend chiefly to the latter. This faculty is now mentioned merely as another part in the inward frame of man, pointing out to us in some degree what we are intended for, and as what will naturally and of course have some influence. The particular place assigned to it by nature, what authority it has, and how great influence it ought to have, shall be hereafter considered.

From this comparison of benevolence and self-love, of our public and private affections, of the courses of life they lead to, and of the principle of reflection or conscience as respecting each of them, it is as manifest that *we were made for society, and to promote the happiness of it, as that we were intended to take care of our own life and health and private good.*

And from this whole review must be given a different draught of human nature from what we are often presented with. Mankind are by nature so closely united, there is such a correspondence between the inward sensations of one man and those of another, that disgrace is as much avoided as bodily pain, and to be the object of esteem and love as much desired. as any external goods; and in many particular cases persons are carried on to do good to others, as the end their affection tends to and rests in; and manifest that they find real satisfaction and enjoyment in this course of behaviour. There is such a natural principle of attraction in man towards man that having trod the same tract of land, having breathed in the same climate, barely having been born in the same artificial district or division, becomes the occasion of contracting acquaintances and familiarities many years after; for anything may serve the purpose. Thus relations merely nominal are sought and invented, not by governors, but by the lowest of the people, which are found sufficient to hold mankind together in little fraternities and copartnerships: weak ties indeed, and what may afford fund enough for ridicule, if they are absurdly considered as the real principles of that union: but they are in truth merely the occasions, as anything may be of anything, upon which our nature carries us on according to its own previous bent and bias; which occasions therefore would be nothing at all were there not this prior disposition and bias of nature. Men are so much one body that in a peculiar manner they feel for each other shame, sudden danger, resentment, honour, prosperity, distress; one or another, or all of these, from the social nature in general, from benevolence, upon the occasion of natural relation, acquaintance, protection, dependence; each of these being distinct cements of society. And therefore to have no restraint from, no regard to, others in our behaviour, is the speculative absurdity of considering ourselves as single and independent, as having nothing in our nature which has respect to our fellow-creatures, reduced to action and practice. And this is the same absurdity as to suppose a hand, or any part, to have no natural respect to any other, or to the whole body.

But, allowing all this, it may be asked, "Has not man dispositions and principles within which lead him to do evil to others, as well as to do good? Whence come the many miseries else which men are the authors and instruments of to each other?" These questions, so far as they relate to the foregoing discourse, may be answered by asking, Has not man also dispositions and principles within which lead him to do evil to himself, as well as good? Whence come the many miseries else—sickness, pain, and death—which men are instruments and authors of to themselves?

It may be thought more easy to answer one of these questions than the other, but the answer to both is really the same: that mankind have ungoverned passions which they will gratify at any rate, as well to the injury of others as in contradiction to known private interest: but that as there is no such thing as self-hatred, so neither is there any such thing as ill-will in one man towards another, emulation and resentment being away; whereas there is plainly benevolence or good-will: there is no such thing as love of injustice, oppression, treachery, ingratitude, but only eager desires after such and such external goods; which, according to a very ancient observation, the most abandoned would choose to obtain by innocent means, if they were as easy and as effectual to their end: that even emulation and resentment, by any one who will consider what these passions really are in nature,* will be found nothing to the purpose of this

---

* Emulation is merely the desire and hope of equality with or superiority over others with whom we compare ourselves. There does not appear to be any *other grief* in the natural passion, but only *that want* which is implied in desire. However, this may be so strong as to be the occasion of great *grief*. To desire the attainment of this equality or superiority by the *particular means* of others being brought down to our own level, or below it, is, I think, the distinct notion of envy. From whence it is easy to see that the real end, which the natural passion emulation, and which the unlawful one envy aims at, is exactly the same; namely, that equality or superiority: and

objection; and that the principles and passions in the mind of man, which are distinct both from self-love and benevolence, primarily and most directly lead to right behaviour with regard to others as well as himself, and only secondarily and accidentally to what is evil. Thus, though men, to avoid the shame of one villainy, are sometimes guilty of a greater, yet it is easy to see that the original tendency of shame is to prevent the doing of shameful actions; and its leading men to conceal such actions when done is only in consequence of their being done; *i.e.*, of the passion's not having answered its first end.

If it be said that there are persons in the world who are in great measure without the natural affections towards their fellow-creatures, there are likewise instances of persons without the common natural affections to themselves. But the nature of man is not to be judged of by either of these, but by what appears in the common world, in the bulk of mankind.

I am afraid it would be thought very strange, if to confirm the truth of this account of human nature, and make out the justness of the foregoing comparison, it should be added that from what appears, men in fact as much and as often contradict that *part* of their

---

consequently, that to do mischief is not the end of envy, but merely the means it makes use of to attain its end. As to resentment, see the Eighth Sermon.

nature which respects *self*, and which leads them to their *own private* good and happiness, as they contradict that *part* of it which respects *society*, and tends to *public* good: that there are as few persons who attain the greatest satisfaction and enjoyment which they might attain in the present world, as who do the greatest good to others which they might do; nay, that there are as few who can be said really and in earnest to aim at one as at the other. Take a survey of mankind: the world in general, the good and bad, almost without exception, equally are agreed that were religion out of the case, the happiness of the present life would consist in a manner wholly in riches, honours, sensual gratifications; insomuch that one scarce hears a reflection made upon prudence, life, conduct, but upon this supposition. Yet, on the contrary, that persons in the greatest affluence of fortune are no happier than such as have only a competency; that the cares and disappointments of ambition for the most part far exceed the satisfactions of it; as also the miserable intervals of intemperance and excess, and the many untimely deaths occasioned by a dissolute course of life: these things are all seen, acknowledged, by every one acknowledged; but are thought no objections against, though they expressly contradict, this universal principle—that the happiness of the present life consists in one or other of them. Whence is all this absurdity and contradiction? Is not the middle way obvious? Can anything be more manifest than that the happiness of life consists in these possessed and enjoyed only to a certain degree; that to pursue them beyond this degree is always attended with more inconvenience than advantage to a man's self, and often with extreme misery and unhappiness? Whence, then, I say, is all this absurdity and contradiction? Is it really the result of consideration in mankind, how they may become most easy to themselves, most free from care, and enjoy the chief happiness attainable in this world? Or is it not manifestly owing either to this, that they have not cool and reasonable concern enough for themselves to consider wherein their chief happiness in the present life consists; or else, if they do consider it, that they will not act conformably to what is the result of that consideration — *i.e.*, reasonable concern for themselves, or cool self-love, is prevailed over by passion and appetite? So that from what appears there is no ground to assert that those principles in the nature of man, which most directly lead to promote the good of our fellow-creatures, are more generally or in a greater degree violated than those which most directly lead us to promote our own private good and happiness.

The sum of the whole is plainly this: The nature of man considered in his single capacity, and with respect only to the present world, is adapted and leads him to attain the greatest happiness he can for himself in the present world. The nature of man considered in his public or social capacity leads him to a right behaviour in society, to that course of life which we call virtue. Men follow or obey their nature in both these capacities and respects to a certain degree, but not entirely: their actions do not come up to the whole of what their nature leads them to in either of these capacities or respects: and they often violate their nature in both; *i.e.*, as they neglect the duties they owe to their fellow-creatures, to which their nature leads them, and are injurious, to which their nature is abhorrent, so there is a manifest negligence in men of their real happiness or interest in the present world, when that interest is inconsistent with a present gratification; for the sake of which they negligently, nay, even knowingly, are the authors and instruments of their own misery and ruin. Thus they are as often unjust to themselves as to others, and for the most part are equally so to both by the same actions.

SERMON II., III.

UPON HUMAN NATURE.

ROMANS ii. 14.

For when the Gentiles, which have not the law, do by nature the things contained in the law, these, having not the law, are a law unto themselves.

As speculative truth admits of different kinds of proof, so likewise moral obligations may be shown by different methods. If the real nature of any creature leads him and is adapted to such and such purposes only, or more than to any other, this is a reason to believe the Author of that nature intended it for those purposes. Thus there is no doubt the eye was intended for us to see with. And the more complex any constitution is, and the greater variety of parts there are which thus tend to some one end, the stronger is the proof that such end was designed. However, when the inward frame of man is considered as any guide in morals, the utmost caution must be used that none make peculiarities in their own temper, or anything which is the effect of particular customs, though observable in several, the standard of what is common to the species; and above all, that the highest principle be not forgot or excluded, that to which belongs the adjustment and correction of all other inward movements and affections; which principle will of course have some influence, but which being in nature supreme, as shall now be shown, ought to preside over and govern all the rest. The difficulty of rightly observing the two former cautions; the appearance there is of some small diversity amongst mankind with respect to this faculty, with respect to their natural sense of moral good and evil; and the attention necessary to survey with any exactness what passes within, have occasioned that it is not so much agreed what is the standard of the internal nature of man as of his external form. Neither is this last exactly settled. Yet we understand one another when we speak of the shape of a human body: so likewise we do when we speak of the heart and inward principles, how far soever the standard is from being exact or precisely fixed. There is therefore ground for an attempt of showing men to themselves, of showing them what course of life and behaviour their real nature points out and would lead them to. Now obligations of virtue shown, and motives to the practice of it enforced, from a review of the nature of man, are to be considered as an appeal to each particular person's heart and natural conscience: as the external senses are appealed to for the proof of things cognisable by them. Since, then, our inward feelings, and the perceptions we receive from our external senses, are equally real, to argue from the former to life and conduct is as little liable to exception as to argue from the latter to absolute speculative truth. A man can as little doubt whether his eyes were given him to see with as he can doubt of the truth of the science of *optics*, deduced from ocular experiments. And allowing the inward feeling, shame, a man can as little doubt whether it was given him to prevent his doing shameful actions as he can doubt whether his eyes were given him to guide his steps. And as to these inward feelings themselves, that they are real, that man has in his nature passions and affections, can no more be questioned than that he has external senses. Neither can the former be wholly mistaken, though to a certain degree liable to greater mistakes than the latter.

There can be no doubt but that several propensions or instincts, several principles in the heart of man, carry him to society, and to contribute to the happiness of it, in a sense and a manner in which no inward principle leads him to evil. These principles, propensions, or instincts which lead him to do good are approved of by a certain faculty within, quite distinct from these propensions themselves. All this hath been fully made out in the foregoing discourse.

But it may be said, "What is all this, though true, to the purpose of virtue and religion? these require, not only that we do good to others when we are led this way, by benevolence or reflection happening to be stronger than other principles, passions, or appetites, but likewise that the *whole* character be formed upon thought and reflection ; that *every* action be directed by some determinate rule, some other rule than the strength and prevalency of any principle or passion. What sign is there in our nature (for the inquiry is only about what is to be collected from thence) that this was intended by its Author? Or how does so various and fickle a temper as that of man appear adapted thereto? It may indeed be absurd and unnatural for men to act without any reflection; nay, without regard to that particular kind of reflection which you call conscience, because this does belong to our nature. For as there never was a man but who approved one place, prospect, building, before another, so it does not appear that there ever was a man who would not have have approved an action of humanity rather than of cruelty; interest and passion being quite out of the case. But interest and passion do come in, and are often too strong for and prevail over reflection and conscience. Now as brutes have various instincts, by which they are carried on to the end the Author of their nature intended them for, is not man in the same condition—with this difference only, that to his instincts (*i.e.*, appetites and passion) is added the principle of reflection or conscience? And as brutes act agreeably to their nature, in following that principle or particular instinct which for the present is strongest in them, does not man likewise act agreeably to his nature, or obey the law of his creation, by following that principle, be it passion or conscience, which for the present happens to be strongest in him? Thus different men are by their particular nature hurried on to pursue honour or riches or pleasure; there are also persons whose temper leads them in an uncommon degree to kindness, compassion, doing good to their fellow-creatures, as there are others who are given to suspend their judgment, to weigh and consider things, and to act upon thought and reflection. Let every one, then, quietly follow his nature, as passion, reflection, appetite, the several parts of it, happen to be strongest; but let not the man of virtue take upon him to blame the ambitious, the covetous, the dissolute, since these equally with him obey and follow their nature. Thus, as in some cases we follow our nature in doing the works *contained in the law,* so in other cases we follow nature in doing contrary."

Now all this licentious talk entirely goes upon a supposition that men follow their nature in the same sense, in violating the known rules of justice and honesty for the sake of a present gratification, as they do in following those rules when they have no temptation to the contrary. And if this were true, that could not be so which St. Paul asserts, that men are *by nature a law to themselves.* If by following nature were meant only acting as we please, it would indeed be ridiculous to speak of nature as any guide in morals; nay, the very mention of deviating from nature would be absurd; and the mention of following it, when spoken by way of distinction, would absolutely have no meaning. For did ever any one act otherwise than as he pleased? And yet the ancients speak of deviating from nature as vice, and of following nature so much as a distinction, that according to them the perfection of virtue consists therein. So that language itself should teach people another sense to the words *following nature* than barely acting as we please. Let it, however, be observed that though the words *human nature* are to be explained, yet the real question of this discourse is not concerning the meaning of words, any other than as the explanation of them may be needful to make out and explain the assertion, that *every man is naturally a law to himself*, that *every one may find within himself the rule of right, and obligations to follow it.* This St. Paul affirms in the words of the text, and this the foregoing objection really denies by seeming to allow it. And the objection will be fully answered, and the text before us explained, by observing that *nature* is considered in different views, and the word used in different senses; and by showing in what view it is considered, and in what sense the word is used, when intended to express and signify that which is the guide of life, that by which men are a law to themselves.* I say, the explanation of the term will be sufficient, because from thence it will appear that in some senses of the word *nature* cannot be, but that in another sense it manifestly is, a law to us.

I. By nature is often meant no more than some principle in man, without regard either to the kind or degree of it. Thus the passion of anger, and the affection of parents to their children, would be called equally *natural*. And as the same person hath often contrary principles, which at the same time draw contrary ways, he may by the same action both follow and contradict his nature in this sense of the word; he may follow one passion and contradict another.

II. *Nature* is frequently spoken of as consisting in those passions which are strongest, and most influence the actions; which being vicious ones, mankind is in this sense naturally vicious, or vicious by nature. Thus St. Paul says of the Gentiles, *who were dead in trespasses and sins, and walked according to the spirit of disobedience, that they were by nature the children of wrath.** They could be no otherwise *children of wrath* by nature than they were vicious by nature.

Here, then, are two different senses of the word

* Ephes. ii. 3.

nature, in neither of which men can at all be said to be a law to themselves. They are mentioned only to be excluded, to prevent their being confounded, as the latter is in the objection, with another sense of it, which is now to be inquired after and explained.

III. The apostle asserts that the Gentiles *do by NATURE the things contained in the law.* Nature is indeed here put by way of distinction from revelation, but yet it is not a mere negative. He intends to express more than that by which they *did not*, that by which they *did*, the works of the law; namely, by *nature*. It is plain the meaning of the word is not the same in this passage as in the former, where it is spoken of as evil; for in this latter it is spoken of as good—as that by which they acted, or might have acted, virtuously. What that is in man by which he is *naturally a law to himself* is explained in the following words: *Which show the work of the law written in their hearts, their consciences also bearing witness, and their thoughts the meanwhile accusing or else excusing one another.* If there be a distinction to be made between the *works written in their hearts*, and the *witness of conscience*, by the former must be meant the natural disposition to kindness and compassion to do what is of good report, to which this apostle often refers: that part of the nature of man, treated of in the foregoing discourse, which with very little reflection and of course leads him to society, and by means of which he naturally acts a just and good part in it, unless other passions or interest lead him astray. Yet since other passions, and regards to private interest, which lead us (though indirectly, yet they lead us) astray, are themselves in a degree equally natural, and often most prevalent, and since we have no method of seeing the particular degrees in which one or the other is placed in us by nature, it is plain the former, considered merely as natural, good and right as they are, can no more be a law to us than the latter. But there is a superior principle of reflection or conscience in every man, which distinguishes between the internal principles of his heart, as well as his external actions; which passes judgment upon himself and them, pronounces determinately some actions to be in themselves just, right, good, others to be in themselves evil, wrong, unjust: which, without being consulted, without being advised with, magisterially exerts itself, and approves or condemns him the doer of them accordingly: and which, if not forcibly stopped, naturally and always of course goes on to anticipate a higher and more effectual sentence, which shall hereafter second and affirm its own. But this part of the office of conscience is beyond my present design explicitly to consider. It is by this faculty, natural to man, that he is a moral agent, that he is a law to himself, but this faculty, I say, not to be considered merely as a principle in his heart, which is to have some influence as well as others, but considered as a faculty in kind and in nature supreme over all others, and which bears its own authority of being so.

This *prerogative*, this *natural supremacy*, of the faculty which surveys, approves, or disapproves the several affections of our mind and actions of our lives, being that by which men *are a law to themselves*, their conformity or disobedience to which law of our nature renders their actions, in the highest and most proper sense, natural or unnatural, it is fit it be further explained to you; and I hope it will be so, if you will attend to the following reflections.

Man may act according to that principle or inclination which for the present happens to be strongest, and yet act in a way disproportionate to, and violate his real proper nature. Suppose a brute creature by any bait to be allured into a snare, by which he is destroyed. He plainly followed the bent of his nature, leading him to gratify his appetite: there is an entire correspondence between his whole nature and such an action: such action therefore is natural. But suppose a man, foreseeing the same danger of certain ruin, should rush into it for the sake of a present gratification; he in this instance would follow his strongest desire, as did the brute creature; but there would be as manifest a disproportion between the nature of a man and such an action as between the meanest work of art and the skill of the greatest master in that art; which disproportion arises, not from considering the action singly in *itself*, or in its *consequences*, but from *comparison* of it with the nature of the agent. And since such an action is utterly disproportionate to the nature of man, it is in the strictest and most proper sense unnatural; this word expressing that disproportion. Therefore, instead of the words *disproportionate to his nature*, the word *unnatural* may now be put; this being more familiar to us: but let it be observed that it stands for the same thing precisely.

Now what is it which renders such a rash action unnatural? Is it that he went against the principle of reasonable and cool self-love, considered *merely* as a part of his nature? No; for if he had acted the contrary way, he would equally have gone against a principle, or part of his nature—namely, passion or appetite. But to deny a present appetite, from foresight that the gratification of it would end in immediate ruin or extreme misery, is by no means an unnatural action: whereas to contradict or go against cool self-love for the sake of such gratification is so in the instance before us. Such an action then being unnatural, and its being so not arising from a man's going against a principle or desire barely, nor in going against that principle or desire which happens for the present to be strongest, it necessarily follows that there must be some other difference or distinction to be made between these two principles, passion and cool self-love, than what I have yet taken notice of. And this difference, not being a difference in strength or degree, I call a difference in *nature* and in *kind*. And since, in the instance still before us, if passion prevails over self-love the consequent action is unnatural, but if self-love prevails over passion the action is natural, it is manifest that self-love is in human nature a superior principle to passion. This may be contradicted without violating that nature; but the former cannot. So that, if we will act conformably to the economy of man's nature, reasonable self-love must govern. Thus, without particular consideration of conscience, we may have a clear conception of the *superior nature* of one inward principle to another, and see that there really is this natural superiority, quite distinct from degrees of strength and prevalency.

Let us now take a view of the nature of man, as consisting partly of various appetites, passions, affections, and partly of the principle of reflection or conscience, leaving quite out all consideration of the different degrees of strength in which either of them prevails, and it will further appear that there is this natural superiority of one inward principle to another, and that it is even part of the idea of reflection or conscience.

Passion or appetite implies a direct simple tendency towards such and such objects, without distinction of the means by which they are to be obtained. Consequently it will often happen there will be a desire of particular objects, in cases where they cannot be obtained without manifest injury to others. Reflection or conscience comes in, and disapproves the pursuit of them in these circumstances; but the desire remains. Which is to be obeyed, appetite or reflection? Cannot this question be answered, from the economy and constitution of human nature merely, without saying which is strongest? Or need this at all come into consideration? Would not the question be *intelligibly* and fully answered by saying that the principle of reflection or conscience being compared with the various appetites, passions, and affections in men, the former is manifestly superior and chief, without regard to strength? And how often soever the latter happens to prevail, it is mere *usurpation*: the former remains in nature and in kind its superior; and every instance of such prevalence of the latter is an instance of breaking in upon and violation of the constitution of man.

All this is no more than the distinction, which everybody is acquainted with, between *mere power* and *authority*: only instead of being intended to express the difference between what is possible and what is lawful in civil government, here it has been shown applicable to the several principles in the mind of man. Thus that principle by which we survey, and either approve or disapprove our own heart, temper, and actions, is not only to be considered as what is in its turn to have some influence—which may be said of every passion, of the lowest appetites—but likewise as being superior, as from its very nature manifestly claiming superiority over all others, insomuch that you cannot form a notion of this faculty, conscience, without taking in judgment, direction, superintendency. This is a constituent part of the idea—that is, of the faculty itself; and to preside and govern, from the very economy and constitution of man, belongs to it. Had it strength, as it had right; had it power, as it had manifest authority, it would absolutely govern the world.

This gives us a further view of the nature of man; shows us what course of life we were made for: not only that our real nature leads us to be influenced in some degree by reflection and conscience, but likewise in what degree we are to be influenced by it, if we will fall in with, and act agreeably to, the constitution of our nature: that this faculty was placed within to be our proper governor, to direct and regulate all under principles, passions, and motives of action. This is its right and office: thus sacred is its authority. And how often soever men violate and rebelliously refuse to submit to it, for supposed interest which they cannot otherwise obtain, or for the sake of passion which they cannot otherwise gratify—this makes no alteration as to the *natural right* and *office* of conscience.

Let us now turn this whole matter another way, and suppose there was no such thing at all as this natural supremacy of conscience—that there was no distinction to be made between one inward principle and another, but only that of strength—and see what would be the consequence.

Consider, then, what is the latitude and compass of the actions of man with regard to himself, his fellow-creatures, and the Supreme Being? What are their bounds, besides that of our natural power? With respect to the two first, they are plainly no other than these: no man seeks misery, as such, for himself; and no one unprovoked does mischief to another for its own sake. For in every degree within these bounds, mankind knowingly, from passion or wantonness, bring ruin and misery upon themselves and others. And impiety and profaneness—I mean what every one would call so who believes the being of God — have absolutely no bounds at all. Men blaspheme the Author of nature, formally and in words renounce their allegiance to their Creator. Put an instance, then, with respect to any one of these three. Though we should suppose profane swearing, and in general that kind of impiety now mentioned, to mean nothing, yet it implies wanton disregard and irreverence towards an infinite Being our Creator; and is this as suitable to the nature of man as reverence and dutiful submission of heart towards that Almighty Being? Or suppose a man guilty of parricide, with all the circumstances of cruelty which such an action can admit of. This action is done in consequence of its principle being for the present strongest; and if there be no difference between inward principles, but only that of strength, the strength being given you have the whole nature of the man given, so far as it relates to this matter. The action plainly corresponds to the principle, the principle being in that degree of strength it was: it therefore corresponds to the whole nature of the man. Upon comparing the action and the whole nature, there arises no disproportion, there appears no unsuitableness, between them. Thus the *murder of a father* and the *nature of man* correspond to each other, as the same nature and an act of filial duty. If there be no difference between inward principles, but only that of strength, we can make no distinction between these two actions, considered as the actions of such a creature; but in our coolest hours must approve or disapprove them equally: than which nothing can be reduced to a greater absurdity.

SERMON III.

The natural supremacy of reflection or conscience being thus established, we may from it form a distinct notion of what is meant by *human nature* when virtue is said to consist in following it, and vice in deviating from it.

As the idea of a civil constitution implies in it united strength, various subordinations under one direction—that of the supreme authority—the different strength of each particular member of the society not coming into the idea—whereas, if you leave out the subordination, the union, and the one direction, you destroy and lose it—so reason, several appetites, passions, and affections, prevailing in different degrees of strength, is not *that* idea or notion of *human nature*; but *that nature* consists in these several principles considered as having a natural respect to each other, in the several passions being naturally subordinate to the one superior principle of reflection or conscience. Every bias, instinct, propension within, is a natural part of our nature, but not the whole: add to these the superior faculty whose office it is to adjust, manage, and preside over them, and take in this its natural superiority, and you complete the idea of human nature. And as in civil government the constitution is broken in upon and violated by power and strength prevailing over authority; so the constitution of man is broken in upon and violated by the lower faculties or principles within prevailing over that which is in its nature supreme over them all. Thus, when it is said by ancient writers that tortures and death are not so contrary to human nature as injustice, by this, to be sure, is not meant that the aversion to the former in mankind is less strong and prevalent than their aversion to the latter, but that the former is only contrary to our nature considered in a partial view, and which takes in only the lowest part of it, that which we have in common with the brutes; whereas the latter is contrary to our nature, considered in a higher sense, as a system and constitution contrary to the whole economy of man.*

* Every man in his physical nature is one individual single agent. He has likewise properties and principles, each of which may be considered separately, and without regard to the respects which they have to each other. Neither of these is the nature we are taking a view of. But it is the inward frame of man considered as a *system* or *constitution*: whose several parts are united, not by a physical principle of individuation, but by the respects they have to each other; the chief of which is the subjection which the appetites, passions, and particular affections have to the one supreme principle of reflection or conscience. The system or constitution is formed by and consists in these respects and this subjection. Thus the body is a *system* or *constitution*: so is a tree; so is every machine. Consider all the several parts of a tree without the natural respects they have to each other, and you have not at all the idea of a tree; but add these respects, and this gives you the idea. The body may be impaired by sickness, a tree may decay, a machine be out of order, and yet the system and constitution of them not totally dissolved. There is plainly somewhat which answers to all this in the moral constitution of man. Whoever will consider his own nature will see that the several appetites, passions, and particular affections have different

And from all these things put together, nothing can be more evident than that, exclusive of revelation, man cannot be considered as a creature left by his Maker to act at random, and live at large up to the extent of his natural power, as passion, humour, wilfulness, happen to carry him, which is the condition brute creatures are in; but that *from his make, constitution, or nature, he is in the strictest and most proper sense a law to himself.* He hath the rule of right within: what is wanting is only that he honestly attend to it.

The inquiries which have been made by men of leisure after some general rule, the conformity to or disagreement from which should denominate our actions good or evil, are in many respects of great

respects amongst themselves. They are restraints upon, and are in a proportion to, each other. This proportion is just and perfect, when all those under principles are perfectly coincident with conscience, so far as their nature permits, and in all cases under its absolute and entire direction. The least excess or defect, the least alteration of the due proportions amongst themselves, or of their coincidence with conscience, though not proceeding into action, is some degree of disorder in the moral constitution. But perfection, though plainly intelligible and unsupposable, was never attained by any man. If the higher principle of reflection maintains its place, and as much as it can corrects that disorder, and hinders it from breaking out into action, this is all that can be expected in such a creature as man. And though the appetites and passions have not their exact due proportion to each other, though they often strive for mastery with judgment or reflection, yet, since the superiority of this principle to all others is the chief respect which forms the constitution, so far as this superiority is maintained, the character, the man, is good, worthy, virtuous.

service. Yet let any plain, honest man, before he engages in any course of action, ask himself, Is this I am going about right, or is it wrong? Is it good, or is it evil? I do not in the least doubt but that this question would be answered agreeably to truth and virtue, by almost any fair man in almost any circumstance. Neither do there appear any cases which look like exceptions to this, but those of superstition, and of partiality to ourselves. Superstition may perhaps be somewhat of an exception; but partiality to ourselves is not, this being itself dishonesty. For a man to judge that to be the equitable, the moderate, the right part for him to act, which he would see to be hard, unjust, oppressive in another, this is plain vice, and can proceed only from great unfairness of mind.

But allowing that mankind hath the rule of right within himself, yet it may be asked, "What obligations are we under to attend to and follow it?" I answer: It has been proved that man by his nature is a law to himself, without the particular distinct consideration of the positive sanctions of that law: the rewards and punishments which we feel, and those which from the light of reason we have ground to believe, are annexed to it. The question, then, carries its own answer along with it. Your obligation to obey this law is its being the law of your nature. That your conscience approves of and attests to such a course of action is itself alone an obligation. Conscience does not only offer itself to show us the way we should walk in, but it likewise carries its own authority with it, that it is our natural guide; the guide assigned us by the Author of our nature: it therefore belongs to our condition of being; it is our duty to walk in that path, and follow this guide, without looking about to see whether we may not possibly forsake them with impunity.

However, let us hear what is to be said against obeying this law of our nature. And the sum is no more than this: "Why should we be concerned about anything out of and beyond ourselves? If we do find within ourselves regards to others, and restraints of we know not how many different kinds, yet these being embarrassments, and hindering us from going the nearest way to our own good, why should we not endeavour to suppress and get over them?"

Thus people go on with words, which when applied to human nature, and the condition in which it is placed in this world, have really no meaning. For does not all this kind of talk go upon supposition, that our happiness in this world consists in somewhat quite distinct from regard to others, and that it is the privilege of vice to be without restraint or confinement? Whereas, on the contrary, the enjoyments—in a manner all the common enjoyments of life, even the pleasures of vice—depend upon these regards of one kind or another to our fellow-creatures. Throw off all regards to others, and we should be quite indifferent to infamy and to honour; there could be no such thing at all as ambition; and scarce any such thing as covetousness; for we should likewise be equally indifferent to the disgrace of poverty, the several neglects and kinds of contempt which accompany this state, and to the reputation of riches, the regard and respect they usually procure. Neither is restraint by any means peculiar to one course of life; but our very nature, exclusive of conscience and our condition, lays us under an absolute necessity of it. We cannot gain any end whatever without being confined to the proper means, which is often the most painful and uneasy confinement. And in numberless instances a present appetite cannot be gratified without such apparent and immediate ruin and misery that the most dissolute man in the world chooses to forego the pleasure rather than endure the pain.

Is the meaning, then, to indulge those regards to our fellow-creatures, and submit to those restraints which upon the whole are attended with more satisfaction than uneasiness, and get over only those which bring more uneasiness and inconvenience than satisfaction? "Doubtless this was our meaning." You have changed sides then. Keep to this; be consistent with yourselves, and you and the men of virtue are *in general* perfectly agreed. But let us take care and avoid mistakes. Let it not be taken for granted that the temper of envy, rage, resentment, yields greater delight than meekness, forgiveness, compassion, and good-will; especially when it is acknowledged that rage, envy, resentment, are in themselves mere misery; and that satisfaction arising from the indulgence of them is little more than relief from that misery; whereas the temper of compassion and benevolence is itself delightful; and the indulgence of it, by doing good, affords new positive delight and enjoyment. Let it not be taken for granted that the satisfaction arising from the reputation of riches and power, however obtained, and from the respect paid to them, is greater than the satisfaction arising from the reputation of justice, honesty, charity, and the esteem which is universally acknowledged to be their due. And if it be doubtful which of these satisfactions is the greatest, as there are persons who think neither of them very considerable, yet there can be no doubt concerning ambition and covetousness, virtue and a good mind, considered in themselves, and as leading to different courses of life; there can, I say, be no doubt, which temper and which course is attended with most peace and tranquillity of mind, which with most perplexity, vexation, and inconvenience. And both the virtues and vices which have been now mentioned, do in a manner equally imply in them regards of one kind or another to our fellow-creatures. And with respect to restraint and confinement, whoever will consider the restraints from fear and shame, the dissimulation, mean arts of concealment, servile compliances, one or other of which belong to almost every course of vice, will soon be convinced that the man of virtue is by no means upon a disadvantage in this respect. How many instances are there in which men feel and own and cry aloud under the chains of vice with which they are enthralled, and which yet they will not shake off! How many instances, in which persons manifestly go through more pains and self-denial to gratify a vicious passion, than would have been necessary to the conquest of it! To this is to be added, that when virtue is become habitual, when the temper of it is acquired, what was before confinement ceases to be so by becoming choice and delight. Whatever restraint and guard upon ourselves may be needful to unlearn any unnatural distortion or odd gesture, yet in all propriety of speech, natural behaviour must be the most easy and unrestrained. It is manifest that, in the common course of life, there is seldom any inconsistency between our duty and what is *called* interest: it is much seldomer that there is an inconsistency between duty and what is really our present interest; meaning by interest, happiness and satisfaction. Self-love, then, though confined to the interest of the present world, does in general perfectly coincide with virtue, and leads us to one and the same course of life. But, whatever exceptions there are to this, which are much fewer than they are commonly thought, all shall be set right at the final distribution of things. It is a manifest absurdity to suppose evil prevailing finally over good, under the conduct and administration of a perfect mind.

The whole argument, which I have been now insisting upon, may be thus summed up, and given you in one view. The nature of man is adapted to some course of action or other. Upon comparing some actions with this nature, they appear suitable and correspondent to it: from comparison of other actions with the same nature, there arises to our view some unsuitableness or disproportion. The correspondence of actions to the nature of the agent renders them natural; their disproportion to it, unnatural. That an action is correspondent to the nature of the agent does not arise from its being agreeable to the principle which happens to be the strongest: for it may be so and yet be quite disproportinate to the nature of the agent. The correspondence therefore, or disproportion, arises from somewhat else. This can be nothing but a difference in nature and kind, altogether distinct from strength, between the inward principles. Some then are in nature and kind superior to others. And the correspondence arises from the action being conformable to the higher principle; and the unsuitableness from its being contrary to it. Reasonable self-love and conscience are the chief or superior principles in the nature of man; because an action may be suitable to this nature, though all other principles be violated, but becomes unsuitable if either of those are. Conscience and self-love, if we understand our true happiness, always lead us the same way. Duty and interest are perfectly coincident; for the most part in this world, but entirely and in every instance if we take in the future and the whole; this being implied in the notion of a good and perfect administration of things. Thus they who have been so wise in their generation as to regard only their own supposed interest, at the expense and to the injury of others, shall at last find, that he who has given up all the advantages of the present world, rather than violate his conscience and the relations of life, has infinitely better provided for himself, and secured his own interest and happiness.

SERMON IV.

UPON THE GOVERNMENT OF THE TONGUE.

JAMES i. 26.

If any man among you seem to be religious, and bridleth not his tongue, but deceiveth his own heart, this man's religion is vain.

THE translation of this text would be more determinate by being more literal, thus: *If any man among you seemeth to be religious, not bridling his tongue, but deceiving his own heart, this man's religion is vain.* This determines that the words, *but deceiveth his own heart*, are not put in opposition to *seemeth to be religious*, but to *bridleth not his tongue.* The certain determinate meaning of the text then being, that he who seemeth to be religious, and bridleth not his tongue, but in that particular deceiveth his own heart, this man's religion is vain, we may observe somewhat very forcible and expressive in these words of St. James. As if the apostle had said, No man surely can make any pretences to religion, who does not at least believe that he bridleth his tongue: if he puts on any appearance or face of religion, and yet does not govern his tongue, he must surely deceive himself in

UPON THE GOVERNMENT OF THE TONGUE.

that particular, and think he does; and whoever is so unhappy as to deceive himself in this, to imagine he keeps that unruly faculty in due subjection when indeed he does not, whatever the other part of his life be, his religion is vain; the government of the tongue being a most material restraint which virtue lays us under: without it no man can be truly religious.

In treating upon this subject, I will consider,

First, what is the general vice or fault here referred to; or what disposition in men is supposed in moral reflections and precepts concerning *bridling the tongue.*

Secondly, when it may be said of any one, that he has a due government over himself in this respect.

I. Now, the fault referred to, and the disposition supposed, in precepts and reflections concerning the government of the tongue, is not evil-speaking from malice, nor lying or bearing false witness from indirect selfish designs. The disposition to these, and the actual vices themselves, all come under other subjects. The tongue may be employed about, and made to serve all the purposes of vice, in tempting and deceiving, in perjury and injustice. But the thing here supposed and referred to, is talkativeness: a disposition to be talking, abstracted from the consideration of what is to be said; with very little or no regard to, or thought of doing, either good or harm. And let not any imagine this to be a slight matter, and that it deserves not to have so great weight laid upon it, till he has considered what evil is implied in it, and the bad effects which follow from it. It is perhaps true, that they who are addicted to this folly would choose to confine themselves to trifles and indifferent subjects, and so intend only to be guilty of being impertinent: but as they cannot go on for ever talking of nothing, as common matters will not afford a sufficient fund for perpetual continued discourse, when subjects of this kind are exhausted they will go on to defamation, scandal, divulging of secrets, their own secrets as well as those of others—anything rather than be silent. They are plainly hurried on in the heat of their talk to say quite different things from what they first intended, and which they afterwards wish unsaid: or improper things, which they had no other end in saying, but only to afford employment to their tongue. And if these people expect to be heard and regarded—for there are some content merely with talking—they will invent to engage your attention: and, when they have heard the least imperfect hint of an affair, they will out of their own head add the circumstances of time and place, and other matters to make out their story and give the appearance of probability to it: not that they have any concern about being believed, otherwise than as a means of being heard. The thing is, to engage your attention; to take you up wholly for the present time: what reflections will be made afterwards, is in truth the least of their thoughts. And further, when persons who indulge themselves in these liberties of the tongue are in any degree offended with another— as little disgusts and misunderstandings will be—they allow themselves to defame and revile such a one without any moderation or bounds; though the offence is so very slight, that they themselves would not do, nor perhaps wish him, an injury in any other way. And in this case the scandal and revilings are chiefly owing to talkativeness, and not bridling their tongue, and so come under our present subject. The least occasion in the world will make the humour break out in this particular way, or in another. It is like a torrent, which must and will flow; but the least thing imaginable will first of all give it either this or another direction, turn it into this or that channel: or like a fire—the nature of which, when in a heap of combustible matter, is to spread and lay waste all around; but any one of a thousand little accidents will occasion it to break out first either in this or another particular part.

The subject then before us, though it does run up into, and can scarce be treated as entirely distinct from all others, yet it needs not be so much mixed or blended with them as it often is. Every faculty and power may be used as the instrument of premeditated vice and wickedness, merely as the most proper and effectual means of executing such designs. But if a man, from deep malice and desire of revenge, should meditate a falsehood with a settled design to ruin his neighbour's reputation, and should with great coolness and deliberation spread it, nobody would choose to say of such a one that he had no government of his tongue. A man may use the faculty of speech as an instrument of false witness, who yet has so entire a command over that faculty as never to speak but from forethought and cool design. Here the crime is injustice and perjury, and, strictly speaking, no more belongs to the present subject than perjury and injustice in any other way. But there is such a thing as a disposition to be talking for its own sake; from which persons often say anything, good or bad, of others, merely as a subject of discourse, according to the particular temper they themselves happen to be in, and to pass away the present time. There is likewise to be observed in persons such a strong and eager desire of engaging attention to what they say, that they will speak good or evil, truth or otherwise, merely as one or the other seems to be most hearkened to: and this, though it is sometimes joined, is not the same with the desire of being thought important and men of consequence. There is in some such a disposition to be talking, that an offence of the slightest kind, and such as would not raise any other resentment, yet raises, if I may so speak, the resentment of the tongue —puts it into a flame, into the most ungovernable motions. This outrage, when the person it respects is present, we distinguish in the lower rank of people by a peculiar term: and let it be observed, that though the decencies of behaviour are a little kept, the same outrage and virulence, indulged when he is absent, is an offence of the same kind. But, not to distinguish any further in this manner, men run into faults and follies which cannot so properly be referred to any one general head as this—that they have not a due government over their tongue.

And this unrestrained volubility and wantonness of speech is the occasion of numberless evils and vexations in life. It begets resentment in him who is the subject of it, sows the seed of strife and dissension amongst others, and inflames little disgusts and offences which if let alone would wear away of themselves: it is often of as bad effect upon the good name of others, as deep envy or malice: and to say the least of it in this respect, it destroys and perverts a certain equity of the utmost importance to society to be observed— namely, that praise and dispraise, a good or bad character, should always be bestowed according to desert. The tongue used in such a licentious manner is like a sword in the hand of a madman; it is employed at random, it can scarce possibly do any good, and for the most part does a world of mischief; and implies not only great folly and a trifling spirit, but great viciousness of mind, great indifference to truth and falsity, and to the reputation, welfare, and good of others. So much reason is there for what St. James says of the tongue, *It is a fire, a world of iniquity, it defileth the whole body, setteth on fire the course of nature, and is itself set on fire of hell.** This is the faculty or disposition which we are required to keep a guard upon: these are the vices and follies it runs into when not kept under due restraint.

II. Wherein the due government of the tongue consists, or when it may be said of any one in a moral and religious sense that he *bridleth his tongue*, I come now to consider.

The due and proper use of any natural faculty or power is to be judged of by the end and design for which it was given us. The chief purpose for which the faculty of speech was given to man is plainly that we might communicate our thoughts to each other, in order to carry on the affairs of the world; for business, and for our improvement in knowledge and learning. But the good Author of our nature designed us not only necessaries, but likewise enjoyment and satisfaction, in that being He hath graciously given, and in that condition of life He hath placed us in. There are secondary uses of our faculties: they administer to delight, as well as to necessity; and as they are equally adapted to both, there is no doubt but He intended

* Chap. iii., ver. 6.

them for our gratification as well as for the support and continuance of our being. The secondary use of speech is to please and be entertaining to each other in conversation. This is in every respect allowable and right; it unites men closer in alliances and friendships; gives us a fellow-feeling of the prosperity and unhappiness of each other; and is in several respects serviceable to virtue, and to promote good behaviour in the world. And provided there be not too much time spent in it, if it were considered only in the way of gratification and delight, men must have strange notion of God and of religion to think that He can be offended with it, or that it is any way inconsistent with the strictest virtue. But the truth is, such sort of conversation, though it has no particular good tendency, yet it has a general good one; it is social and friendly, and tends to promote humanity, good-nature, and civility.

As the end and use, so likewise the abuse of speech, relates to the one or other of these: either to business or to conversation. As to the former: deceit in the management of business and affairs does not properly belong to the subject now before us: though one may just mention that multitude, that endless number of words with which business is perplexed, when a much fewer would, as it should seem, better serve the purpose; but this must be left to those who understand the matter. The government of the tongue, considered as a subject of itself, relates chiefly to conversation; to that kind of discourse which usually fills up the time spent in friendly meetings and visits of civility. And the danger is, lest persons entertain themselves and others at the expense of their wisdom and their virtue, and to the injury or offence of their neighbour. If they will observe and keep clear of these, they may be as free and easy and unreserved as they can desire.

The cautions to be given for avoiding these dangers, and to render conversation innocent and agreeable, fall under the following particulars: silence; talking of indifferent things; and, which makes up too great a part of conversation, giving of characters, speaking well or evil of others.

The Wise Man observes that "there is a time to speak, and a time to keep silence." One meets with people in the world who seem never to have made the last of these observations. And yet these great talkers do not at all speak from their having anything to say, as every sentence shows, but only from their inclination to be talking. Their conversation is merely an exercise of the tongue: no other human faculty has any share in it. It is strange these persons can help reflecting, that unless they have in truth a superior capacity, and are in an extraordinary manner furnished for conversation if they are entertaining, it is at their own expense. Is it possible that it should never come into people's thoughts to suspect whether or no it be to their advantage to show so very much of themselves? "O that you would altogether hold your peace, and it should be your wisdom."* Remember likewise there are persons who love fewer words, an inoffensive sort of people, and who deserve some regard, though of too still and composed tempers for you. Of this number was the Son of Sirach: for he plainly speaks from experience when he says, "As hills of sand are to the steps of the aged, so is one of many words to a quiet man." But one would think it should be obvious to every one, that when they are in company with their superiors of any kind—in years, knowledge, and experience—when proper and useful subjects are discoursed of, which they cannot bear a part in, that these are times for silence, when they should learn to hear, and be attentive, at least in their turn. It is indeed a very unhappy way these people are in; they in a manner cut themselves out from all advantage of conversation, except that of being entertained with their own talk: their business in coming into company not being at all to be informed, to hear, to learn, but to display themselves, or rather to exert their faculty, and talk without any design at all. And if we consider conversation as an entertainment, as somewhat to unbend the mind, as a diversion from the cares, the business, and the sorrows of life, it is of the very nature of it

* Job xiii. 5.

that the discourse be mutual. This, I say, is implied in the very notion of what we distinguish by conversation, or being in company. Attention to the continued discourse of one alone grows more painful, often, than the cares and business we come to be diverted from. He, therefore, who imposes this upon us is guilty of a double offence—arbitrarily enjoining silence upon all the rest, and likewise obliging them to this painful attention.

I am sensible these things are apt to be passed over, as too little to come into a serious discourse; but in reality men are obliged, even in point of morality and virtue, to observe all the decencies of behaviour. The greatest evils in life have had their rise from somewhat which was thought of too little importance to be attended to. And as to the matter we are now upon, it is absolutely necessary to be considered. For if people will not maintain a due government over themselves, in regarding proper times and seasons for silence, but *will* be talking, they certainly, whether they design it or not at first, will go on to scandal and evil-speaking, and divulging secrets.

If it were needful to say anything further to persuade men to learn this lesson of silence, one might put them in mind how insignificant they render themselves by this excessive talkativeness: insomuch that, if they do chance to say anything which deserves to be attended to and regarded, it is lost in the variety and abundance which they utter of another sort.

The occasions of silence then are obvious, and one would think should be easily distinguished by everybody: namely, when a man has nothing to say; or nothing but what is better unsaid: better, either in regard to the particular persons he is present with; or from its being an interruption to conversation itself; or to conversation of a more agreeable kind; or better, lastly, with regard to himself. I will end this particular with two reflections of the Wise Man; one of which, in the strongest manner, exposes the ridiculous part of this licentiousness of the tongue; and the other, the great danger and viciousness of it. *When he that is a fool walketh by the way side, his wisdom faileth him, and he saith to every one that he is a fool.** The other is, *In the multitude of words there wanteth not sin.*†

As to the government of the tongue in respect to talking upon indifferent subjects: after what has been said concerning the due government of it in respect to the occasions and times for silence, there is little more necessary than only to caution men to be fully satisfied that the subjects are indeed of an indifferent nature; and not to spend too much time in conversation of this kind. But persons must be sure to take heed that the subject of their discourse be at least of an

* Eccles. x. 3.   † Prov. x 19.

indifferent nature : that it be no way offensive to virtue, religion, or good manners : that it be not of a licentious, dissolute sort, this leaving always ill impressions upon the mind; that it be no way injurious or vexatious to others; and that too much time be not spent this way, to the neglect of those duties and offices of life which belong to their station and condition in the world. However, though there is not any necessity that men should aim at being important and weighty in every sentence they speak : yet since useful subjects, at least of some kinds, are as entertaining as others, a wise man, even when he desires to unbend his mind from business, would choose that the conversation might turn upon somewhat instructive.

The last thing is, the government of the tongue as relating to discourse of the affairs of others, and giving of characters. These are in a manner the same ; and one can scarce call it an indifferent subject, because discourse upon it almost perpetually runs into somewhat criminal.

And, first of all, it were very much to be wished that this did not take up so great a part of conversation; because it is indeed a subject of a dangerous nature. Let any one consider the various interests, competitions, and little misunderstandings which arise amongst men; and he will soon see that he is not unprejudiced and impartial; that he is not, as I may speak, neutral enough to trust himself with talking of the character and concerns of his neighbour, in a free, careless, and unreserved manner. There is perpetually, and often it is not attended to, a rivalship amongst people of one kind or another in respect to wit, beauty, learning, fortune, and that one thing will insensibly influence them to speak to the disadvantage of others, even where there is no formed malice or ill-design. Since therefore it is so hard to enter into this subject without offending, the first thing to be observed is that people should learn to decline it; to get over that strong inclination most have to be talking of the concerns and behaviour of their neighbour.

But since it is impossible that this subject should be wholly excluded conversation; and since it is necessary that the characters of men should be known: the next thing is that it is a matter of importance what is said; and, therefore, that we should be religiously scrupulous and exact to say nothing, either good or bad, but what is true. I put it thus, because it is in reality of as great importance to the good of society, that the characters of bad men should be known, as that the characters of good men should. People who are given to scandal and detraction may indeed make an ill-use of this observation; but truths, which are of service towards regulating our conduct, are not to be disowned, or even concealed, because a bad use may be made of them. This however would be effectually prevented if these two things were attended to. First, That, though it is equally of bad consequence to society that men should have either good or ill characters which they do not deserve; yet, when you say somewhat good of a man which he does not deserve, there is no wrong done him in particular; whereas, when you say evil of a man which he does not deserve, here is a direct formal injury, a real piece of injustice done him. This therefore makes a wide difference; and gives us, in point of virtue, much greater latitude in speaking well than ill of others. Secondly, A good man is friendly to his fellow-creatures, and a lover of mankind; and so will, upon every occasion, and often without any, say all the good he can of everybody; but, so far as he is a good man, will never be disposed to speak evil of any, unless there be some other reason for it, besides, barely that it is true. If he be charged with having given an ill character, he will scarce think it a sufficient justification of himself to say it was a true one, unless he can also give some further account how he came to do so: a just indignation against particular instances of villainy, where they are great and scandalous; or to prevent an innocent man from being deceived and betrayed, when he has great trust and confidence in one who does not deserve it. Justice must be done to every part of a subject when we are considering it. If there be a man, who bears a fair character in the world, whom yet we know to be without faith or honesty, to be really an ill man; it must be allowed in general that we shall do a piece of service to society by letting such a one's true character be known. This is no more than what we have an instance of in our Saviour himself;* though He was mild and gentle beyond example. However, no words can express too strongly the caution which should be used in such a case as this.

Upon the whole matter: If people would observe the obvious occasions of silence, if they would subdue the inclination to talebearing, and that eager desire to engage attention, which is an original disease in some minds, they would be in little danger of offending with their tongue; and would, in a moral and religious sense, have due government over it.

I will conclude with some precepts and reflections of the Son of Sirach upon this subject. *Be swift to hear; and, if thou hast understanding, answer thy neighbour; if not, lay thy hand upon thy mouth. Honour and shame is in talk. A man of an ill tongue is dangerous in his city, and he that is rash in his talk shall be hated. A wise man will hold his tongue till he see opportunity; but a babbler and a fool will regard no time. He that useth many words shall be abhorred; and he that taketh to himself authority therein shall be hated. A backbiting tongue*

* Mark xii. 38, 40.

hath disquieted many; strong cities hath it pulled down, and overthrown the houses of great men. The tongue of a man is his fall; but if thou love to hear, thou shalt receive understanding.

SERMON V.

UPON COMPASSION.

Rom. xii. 15.

Rejoice with them that do rejoice, and weep with them that weep.

Every man is to be considered in two capacities, the private and public; as designed to pursue his own interest, and likewise to contribute to the good of others. Whoever will consider may see that, in general, there is no contrariety between these; but that from the original constitution of man, and the circumstances he is placed in, they perfectly coincide, and mutually carry on each other. But, amongst the great variety of affections or principles of action in our nature, some in their primary intention and design seem to belong to the single or private, others to the public or social capacity. The affections required in the text are of the latter sort. When we rejoice in the prosperity of others, and compassionate their distresses, we as it were substitute them for ourselves, their interest for our own; and have the same kind of pleasure in their prosperity, and sorrow in their distress, as we have from reflection upon our own. Now there is nothing strange or unaccountable in our being thus carried out, and affected towards the interests of others. For, if there be any appetite, or any inward principle besides self-love; why may there not be an affection to the good of our fellow-creatures, and delight from that affection's being gratified, and uneasiness from things going contrary to it?*

* There being manifestly this appearance of men's substituting others for themselves, and being carried out and affected towards them as towards themselves; some persons, who have a system which excludes every affection of this sort, have taken a pleasant method to solve it; and tell you it is *not another* you are at all concerned about, but your *self only*, when you feel the affection called compassion, *i.e.* Here is a plain matter of fact, which men cannot reconcile with the general account they think fit to give of things: they therefore, instead of *that* manifest fact, substitute *another*, which is reconcilable to their own scheme. For does not everybody by compassion mean an affection, the object of which is another in distress? Instead of this, but designing to have it mistaken for this, they speak of an affection or passion, the object of which is ourselves, or danger to ourselves. Hobbes defines *pity, imagination, or fiction of future calamity to ourselves, proceeding from the sense* (he means sight or knowledge) *of another man's calamity*. Thus fear and compassion would be the same idea, and a fearful and a compassionate man the same character, which every one immediately sees are totally different. Further, to those who give any scope to their affections, there is no perception or inward feeling more universal than this: that one who has been merciful and compassionate throughout the course of his behaviour should himself be treated with kindness, if he happens to fall into circumstances of distress.

Is fear, then, or cowardice, so great a recommendation to the favour of the bulk of mankind? Or is it not plain that mere fearlessness (and therefore not the contrary) is one of the most popular qualifications? This shows that mankind are not affected towards compassion as fear, but as somewhat totally different.

Nothing would more expose such accounts as these of the affections which are favourable and friendly to our fellow-creatures than to substitute the definitions, which this author, and others who follow

Of these two, delight in the prosperity of others, and compassion for their distresses, the last is felt much more generally than the former. Though men do not universally rejoice with all whom they see rejoice, yet, accidental obstacles removed, they naturally compassionate all, in some degree, whom they see in distress; so far as they have any real perception or sense of that distress: insomuch that words expressing this latter, pity, compassion, frequently occur: whereas we have scarce any single one by which the former is distinctly expressed. Congratulation indeed answers condolence: but both these

---

his steps, give of such affections, instead of the words by which they are commonly expressed. Hobbes, after having laid down. that pity or compassion is only fear for ourselves, goes on to explain the reason why we pity our friends in distress more than others. Now substitute the word *definition* instead of the word *pity* in this place, and the inquiry will be, why we fear our friends, &c., which words (since he really does not mean why we are afraid of them) make no question or sentence at all. So that common language, the words *to compassionate, to pity,* cannot be accommodated to his account of compassion. The very joining of the words to *pity our friends* is a direct contradiction to his definition of pity: because those words, so joined, neccessarily express that our friends are the objects of the passion; whereas his definition of it asserts that ourselves (or danger to ourselves) are the only objects of it. He might indeed have avoided this absurdity, by plainly saying what he is going to account for; namely, why the sight of the innocent, or of our friends in distress, raises greater fear for ourselves than the sight of other persons in distress. But had he put the thing thus plainly, the fact itself would have been doubted; that *the sight of our friends in distress raises in us greater fear for ourselves than the sight of others in distress.* And in the next place it would immediately have occurred to every one that the fact now mentioned, which at least is doubtful whether, true or false, was not the same with this fact, which nobody ever

words are intended to signify certain forms of civility rather than any inward sensation or feeling. This difference or inequality is so remarkable that we plainly consider compassion as itself an original, distinct, particular affection in human nature; whereas to rejoice in the good of others is only a consequence of the general affection of love and good-will to them. The reason and account of which matter is this: when a man has obtained any particular advantage or felicity, his end is gained; and he does not in that particular want the assistance of another: there was therefore no need of a distinct affection towards that

doubted, that *the sight of our friends in distress raises in us greater compassion than the sight of others in distress:* every one, I say, would have seen that these are not the *same*, but *two different* inquiries; and, consequently, that fear and compassion are not the same. Suppose a person to be in real danger, and by some means or other to have forgot it; any trifling accident, any sound might alarm him, recall the danger to his remembrance, and renew his fear; but it is almost too grossly ridiculous (though it is to show an absurdity) to speak of that sound or accident as an object of compassion; and yet, according to Mr. Hobbes, our greatest friend in distress is no more to us, no more the object of compassion, or of any affection in our heart: neither the one nor the other raises any emotion in our mind, but only the thoughts of our liableness to calamity, and the fear of it; and both equally do this. It is fit such sort of accounts of human nature should be shown to be what they really are, because there is raised upon them a general scheme, which undermines the whole foundation of common justice and honesty. See *Hobbes of Human Nature,* c. 9. § 10.

There are often three distinct perceptions or inward feelings upon sight of persons in distress: real sorrow and concern for the misery of our fellow-creatures; some degree of satisfaction from a consciousness of our freedom from that misery; and as the mind passes on from one thing to another, it is not unnatural from such an occasion

felicity of another already obtained; neither would such affection directly carry him on to do good to that person: whereas men in distress want assistance; and compassion leads us directly to assist them. The object of the former is the present felicity of another; the object of the latter is the present misery of another. It is easy to see that the latter wants a particular affection for its relief, and that the former does not want one because it does not want assistance. And upon supposition of a distinct affection in both cases, the one must rest in the exercise of itself, having nothing further to gain; the other does not

<blockquote>
to reflect upon our own liableness to the same or other calamities. The two last frequently accompany the first, but it is the first *only* which is properly compassion, of which the distressed are the objects, and which directly carries us with calmness and thought to their assistance. Any one of these, from various and complicated reasons, may in particular cases prevail over the other two; and there are, I suppose, instances, where the bare *sight* of distress, without our feeling any compassion for it, may be the occasion of either or both of the two latter perceptions. One might add that if there be really any such thing as the fiction or imagination of danger to ourselves from sight of the miseries of others, which Hobbes speaks of, and which he has absurdly mistaken for the whole of compassion; if there be anything of this sort common to mankind, distinct from the reflection of reason, it would be a most remarkable instance of what was furthest from his thoughts—namely, of a mutual sympathy between each particular of the species, a fellow-feeling common to mankind. It would not indeed be an example of our substituting others for ourselves, but it would be an example of our substituting ourselves for others. And as it would not be an instance of benevolence, so neither would it be any instance of self-love: for this phantom of danger to ourselves, naturally rising to view upon sight of the distresses of others, would be no more an instance of love to ourselves than the pain of hunger is.
</blockquote>

rest in itself, but carries us on to assist the distressed.

But, supposing these affections natural to the mind, particularly the last; "Has not each man troubles enough of his own? must he indulge an affection which appropriates to himself those of others? which leads him to contract the least desirable of all friendships, friendships with the unfortunate? Must we invert the known rule of prudence, and choose to associate ourselves with the distressed? or, allowing that we ought, so far as it is in our power to relieve them, yet is it not better to do this from reason and duty? Does not passion and affection of every kind perpetually mislead us? Nay, is not passion and affection itself a weakness, and what a perfect being must be entirely free from?" Perhaps so, but it is mankind I am speaking of; imperfect creatures, and who naturally and, from the condition we are placed in, necessarily depend upon each other. With respect to such creatures, it would be found of as bad consequence to eradicate all natural affections as to be entirely governed by them. This would almost sink us to the condition of brutes; and that would leave us without a sufficient principle of action. Reason alone, whatever any one may wish, is not in reality a sufficient motive of virtue in such a creature as man; but this reason joined with those affections which God has impressed upon his heart, and when these are allowed scope to exercise themselves, but under strict government and direction of reason, then it is we act suitably to our nature, and to the circumstances God has placed us in. Neither is affection itself at all a weakness; nor does it argue defect, any otherwise than as our senses and appetites do; they belong to our condition of nature, and are what we cannot be without. God Almighty is, to be sure, unmoved by passion or appetite, unchanged by affection; but then it is to be added that He neither sees nor hears nor perceives things by any senses like ours; but in a manner infinitely more perfect. Now, as it is an absurdity almost too gross to be mentioned, for a man to endeavour to get rid of his senses, because the Supreme Being discerns things more perfectly without them; it is as real, though not so obvious an absurdity, to endeavour to eradicate the passions He has given us, because He is without them. For, since our passions are as really a part of our constitution as our senses; since the former as really belong to our condition of nature as the latter; to get rid of either is equally a violation of and breaking in upon that nature and constitution He has given us. Both our senses and our passions are a supply to the imperfection of our nature; thus they show that we are such sort of creatures as to stand in need of those helps which higher orders of creatures do not. But it is not the supply, but the deficiency; as it is not a remedy, but a disease, which is the imperfection. However, our appetites, passions, senses, no way imply disease: nor indeed do they imply deficiency or imperfection of any sort; but only this, that the constitution of nature, according to which God has made us, is such as to require them. And it is so far from being true, that a wise man must entirely suppress compassion, and all fellow-feeling for others, as a weakness; and trust to reason alone to teach and enforce upon him the practice of the several charities we owe to our kind; that, on the contrary, even the bare exercise of such affections would itself be for the good and happiness of the world; and the imperfection of the higher principles of reason and religion in man, the little influence they have upon our practice, and the strength and prevalency of contrary ones, plainly require these affections to be a restraint upon these latter, and a supply to the deficiencies of the former.

First, The very exercise itself of these affections in a just and reasonable manner and degree would upon the whole increase the satisfactions and lessen the miseries of life.

It is the tendency and business of virtue and religion to procure, as much as may be, universal good-will, trust, and friendship amongst mankind. If this could be brought to obtain; and each man enjoyed the happiness of others, as every one does that of a friend; and looked upon the success and prosperity of his neighbour as every one does upon that of his children and family; it is too manifest to be insisted upon how much the enjoyments of life would be increased. There would be so much happiness introduced into the world, without any deduction or inconvenience from it, in proportion as the precept of *rejoicing with those who rejoice* was universally obeyed. Our Saviour has owned this good affection as belonging to our nature in the parable of the *lost sheep,* and does not think it to the disadvantage of a perfect state to represent its happiness as capable of increase from reflection upon that of others.

But since in such a creature as man, compassion or sorrow for the distress of others seems so far necessarily connected with joy in their prosperity, as that whoever rejoices in one must unavoidably compassionate the other; there cannot be that delight or satisfaction, which appears to be so considerable, without the inconveniences, whatever they are, of compassion.

However, without considering this connection, there is no doubt but that more good than evil, more delight than sorrow, arises from compassion itself; there being so many things which balance the sorrow of it. There is first the relief which the distressed feel from this affection in others towards them. There is likewise the additional misery which they would feel from the reflection that no one commiserated their case. It is indeed true that any disposition, prevailing beyond a certain degree, becomes somewhat wrong; and we have ways of speaking, which, though they do not directly express that excess, yet always lead our thoughts to it, and give us the notion of it. Thus, when mention is made of delight in being pitied, this always conveys to our mind the notion of somewhat which is really a weakness. The manner of speaking, I say, implies a certain weakness and feebleness of mind, which is and ought to be disapproved. But men of the greatest fortitude would in distress feel uneasiness from knowing that no person in the world had any sort of compassion or real concern for them; and in some cases, especially when the temper is enfeebled by sickness, or any long and great distress, doubtless, would feel a kind of relief even from the helpless goodwill and ineffectual assistances of those about them. Over against the sorrow of compassion is likewise to be set a peculiar calm kind of satisfaction, which accompanies it, unless in cases where the distress of another is by some means so brought home to ourselves as to become in a manner our own; or when from weakness of mind the affection rises too high, which ought to be corrected. This tranquillity, or calm satisfaction, proceeds partly from consciousness of a right affection and temper of mind, and partly from a sense of our own freedom from the misery we compassionate. This last may possibly appear to some at first sight faulty; but it really is not so. It is the same with that positive enjoyment, which sudden ease from pain for the present affords, arising from a real sense of misery, joined with a sense of our freedom from it; which in all cases must afford some degree of satisfaction.

To these things must be added the observation which respects both the affections we are considering; that they who have got over all fellow-feeling for others have withal contracted a certain callousness of heart, which renders them insensible to most other satisfactions but those of the grossest kind.

Secondly, Without the exercise of these affections men would certainly be much more wanting in the offices of charity they owe to each other, and likewise more cruel and injurious than they are at present.

The private interest of the individual would not be sufficiently provided for by reasonable and cool self-love alone; therefore the appetites and passions are placed within as a guard and further security, without which it would not be taken due care of. It is manifest our life would be neglected were it not for the calls of hunger and thirst and weariness; notwithstanding that without them reason would assure us that the recruits of food and sleep are the necessary means of our preservation. It is therefore absurd to imagine that, without affection, the same reason alone would be more effectual to engage us to perform the duties we owe to our fellow-creatures. One of this make would be as defective, as much wanting, considered with respect to society, as one of the former make would be defective, or wanting, considered as an individual, or in his private capacity. Is it possible any can in earnest think that a public spirit, *i.e.*, a settled reasonable principle of benevolence to mankind, is so prevalent and strong in the species as that we may venture to throw off the under affections, which are its assistants, carry it forward and mark out particular courses for it; family, friends, neighbourhood, the distressed, our country? The common joys and the common sorrows, which belong to these relations and circumstances, are as plainly useful to society as the pain and pleasure belonging to hunger, thirst, and weariness are of service to the individual. In defect of that higher principle of reason, compassion is often the only way by which the indigent can have access to us: and therefore, to eradicate this, though it is not indeed formally to deny them that assistance which is their due; yet it is to cut them off from that which is too frequently their only way of obtaining it. And as for those who have shut up this door against the complaints of the miserable, and conquered this affection in themselves; even these persons will be under great restraints from the same affection in others. Thus a man who has himself no sense of injustice, cruelty, oppression, will be kept from running the utmost lengths of wickedness by fear of that detestation, and even resentment of inhumanity, in many particular instances of it, which compassion for the object towards whom such inhumanity is exercised, excites in the bulk of mankind. And this is frequently the chief danger and the chief restraint which tyrants and the great oppressors of the world feel.

In general, experience will show that, as want of natural appetite to food supposes and proceeds from some bodily disease; so the apathy the Stoics talk of as much supposes, or is accompanied with, somewhat amiss in the moral character, in that which is the health of the mind. Those who formerly aimed at this upon the foot of philosophy appear to have had better success in eradicating the affections of tenderness and compassion than they had with the passions of envy, pride, and resentment: these latter, at best, were but concealed, and that imperfectly too. How far this observation may be extended to such as endeavour to suppress the natural impulses of their affections, in order to form themselves for business and the world, I shall not determine. But there does not appear any capacity or relation to be named, in which men ought to be entirely deaf to the calls of affection, unless the judicial one is to be excepted.

And as to those who are commonly called the men of pleasure, it is manifest that the reason they set up for hardness of heart is to avoid being interrupted in their course by the ruin and misery they are the authors of; neither are persons of this character always the most free from the impotencies of envy and resentment. What may men at last bring themselves to, by suppressing their passions and affections of one kind, and leaving those of the other in their full strength? But surely it might be expected that persons who make pleasure their study and their business, if they understood what they profess, would reflect, how many of the entertainments of life, how many of those kind of amusements which seem peculiarly to belong to men of leisure and education they became insensible to by this acquired hardness of heart.

I shall close these reflections with barely mentioning the behaviour of that divine Person, who was the example of all perfection in human nature, as represented in the Gospels mourning, and even, in a literal sense, weeping over the distresses of His creatures.

The observation already made, that, of the two affections mentioned in the text, the latter exerts itself much more than the former; that, from the original constitution of human nature, we much more generally and sensibly compassionate the distressed, than rejoice with the prosperous, requires to be particularly considered. This observation, therefore, with the reflections which arise out of it, and which it leads our thoughts to, shall be the subject of another discourse.

For the conclusion of this, let me just take notice of the danger of over-great refinements; of going beside or beyond the plain, obvious, first appearances of things, upon the subject of morals and religion. The least observation will show how little the generality of men are capable of speculations. Therefore morality and religion must be somewhat plain and easy to be understood: it must appeal to what we call plain common sense, as distinguished from superior capacity and improvement; because it appeals to mankind. Persons of superior capacity and improvement have often fallen into errors which no one of mere common understanding could. Is it possible that one of this latter character could ever of himself have thought that there was absolutely no such thing in mankind as affection to the good of others? suppose of parents to their children; or that what he felt upon seeing a friend in distress was only fear for himself; or, upon supposition of the affections of kindness and compassion, that it was the business of wisdom and virtue to set him about extirpating them as fast as he could? And yet each of these manifest contradictions to nature has been laid down by men of speculation as a discovery in moral philosophy; which they, it seems, have found out through all the specious appearances to the contrary. This reflection may be extended further. The extravagances of enthusiasm and superstition do not at all lie in the road of common sense; and therefore, so far as they are *original mistakes*, must be owing to going beside or beyond it. Now, since inquiry and examination can relate only to things so obscure and uncertain as to stand in need of it, and to persons who are capable of it; the proper advice to be given to plain honest men, to secure them from the extremes both of superstition and irreligion, is that of the Son of Sirach: *In every good work trust thy own soul; for this is the keeping of the commandment.*[*]

[*] Ecclus. xxxii. 23.

SERMON VI.

UPON COMPASSION.

PREACHED THE FIRST SUNDAY IN LENT.

Rom. xii. 15.

Rejoice with them that do rejoice, and weep with them that weep.

THERE is a much more exact correspondence between the natural and moral world than we are apt to take notice of. The inward frame of man does in a peculiar manner answer to the external condition and circumstances of life in which he is placed. This is a particular instance of that general observation of the Son of Sirach: *All things are double one against another, and God hath made nothing imperfect.* * The several passions and affections in the heart of man, compared with the circumstances of life in which he is placed, afford, to such as will attend to them, as certain instances of final causes, as any whatever, which are more commonly alleged for such: since those affections lead him to a certain determinate course of action suitable to those circumstances; as (for instance) compassion to relieve the distressed. And as all observations of final

* Ecclus. xlii. 24.

causes, drawn from the principles of action in the heart of man, compared with the condition he is placed in, serve all the good uses which instances of final causes in the material world about us do; and both these are equally proofs of wisdom and design in the Author of nature: so the former serve to further good purposes; they show us what course of life we are made for, what is our duty, and in a peculiar manner enforce upon us the practice of it.

Suppose we are capable of happiness and of misery in degrees equally intense and extreme, yet, we are capable of the latter for a much longer time, beyond all comparison. We see men in the tortures of pain for hours, days, and, excepting the short suspensions of sleep, for months together, without intermission, to which no enjoyments of life do, in degree and continuance, bear any sort of proportion. And such is our make and that of the world about us that any thing may become the instrument of pain and sorrow to us. Thus almost any one man is capable of doing mischief to any other, though he may not be capable of doing him good; and if he be capable of doing him some good, he is capable of doing him more evil. And it is, in numberless cases, much more in our power to lessen the miseries of others than to promote their positive happiness, any otherwise than as the former often includes the latter; ease from misery occasioning for some time the greatest positive enjoyment.

This constitution of nature, namely, that it is so much more in our power to occasion and likewise to lessen misery than to promote positive happiness, plainly required a particular affection to hinder us from abusing, and to incline us to make a right use of the former powers, *i.e.*, the powers both to occasion and to lessen misery; over and above what was necessary to induce us to make a right use of the latter power, that of promoting positive happiness. The power we have over the misery of our fellow-creatures, to occasion or lessen it, being a more important trust than the power we have of promoting their positive happiness; the former requires and has a further, an additional, security and guard against its being violated, beyond and over and above what the latter has. The social nature of man, and general goodwill to his species, equally prevent him from doing evil, incline him to relieve the distressed, and to promote the positive happiness of his fellow-creatures; but compassion only restrains from the first, and carries him to the second; it hath nothing to do with the third.

The final causes, then, of compassion are to prevent and to relieve misery.

As to the former: this affection may plainly be a restraint upon resentment, envy, unreasonable self-love; that is, upon all the principles from which men do evil to one another. Let us instance only in resentment. It seldom happens, in regulated societies, that men have an enemy so entirely in their power as to be able to satiate their resentment with safety. But if we were to put this case, it is plainly supposable that a person might bring his enemy into such a condition, as from being the object of anger and rage, to become an object of compassion, even to himself, though the most malicious man in the world; and in this case compassion would stop him, if he could stop with safety, from pursuing his revenge any further. But since nature has placed within us more powerful restraints to prevent mischief, and since the final cause of compassion is much more to relieve misery, let us go on to the consideration of it in this view.

As this world was not intended to be a state of any great satisfaction or high enjoyment, so neither was it intended to be a mere scene of unhappiness and sorrow. Mitigations and reliefs are provided by the merciful Author of nature for most of the afflictions in human life. There is kind provision made even against our frailties: as we are so constituted that time abundantly abates our sorrows, and begets in us that resignation of temper, which ought to have been produced by a better cause; a due sense of the authority of God, and our state of dependence. This holds in respect too far the greatest part of the evils of life; I suppose, in some degree, as to pain and sickness. Now this part of the constitution or make of man, considered as some relief to misery, and not as provision for positive happiness, is, if I may so speak, an instance of nature's compassion for us; and every natural remedy or relief to misery may be considered in the same view.

But since in many cases it is very much in our power to alleviate the miseries of each other; and benevolence, though natural in man to man, yet is in a very low degree kept down by interest and competitions; and men, for the most part, are so engaged in the business and pleasures of the world, as to overlook and turn away from objects of misery; which are plainly considered as interruptions to them in their way, as intruders upon their business, their gaiety, and mirth: compassion is an advocate within us in their behalf, to gain the unhappy admittance and access, to make their case attended to. If it sometimes serves a contrary purpose, and makes men industriously turn away from the miserable, these are only instances of abuse and perversion: for the end, for which the affection was given us, most certainly is not to make us avoid, but to make us attend to, the objects of it. And if men would only resolve to allow thus much to it: let it bring before their view, the view of their mind, the miseries of their fellow-creatures; let it gain for them that their case be considered; I am persuaded it would not fail of gaining more, and that very few real objects of charity would pass unrelieved. Pain and sorrow and misery have a right to our assistance: compassion puts us in mind of the debt, and that we owe it to ourselves as well as to the distressed. For, to endeavour to get rid of the sorrow of compassion by turning from the wretched, when yet it is in our power to relieve them, is as unnatural as to endeavour to get rid of the pain of hunger by keeping from the sight of food. That we can do one with greater success than we can the other is no proof that one is less a violation of nature than the other. Compassion is a call, a demand of nature, to relieve the unhappy as hunger is a natural call for food. This affection plainly gives the objects of it an additional claim to relief and mercy, over and above what our fellow-creatures in common have to our goodwill. Liberality and bounty are exceedingly commendable; and a particular distinction in such a world as this, where men set themselves to contract their heart, and close it to all interests but their own. It is by no means to be opposed to mercy, but always accompanies it: the distinction between them is only that the former leads our thoughts to a more promiscuous and undistinguished distribution of favours; to those who are not, as well as those who are, necessitous; whereas the object of compassion is misery. But in the comparison, and where there is not a possibility of both, mercy is to have the preference: the affection of compassion manifestly leads us to this preference. Thus, to relieve the indigent and distressed, to single out the unhappy, from whom can be expected no returns either of present entertainment or future service, for the objects of our favours; to esteem a man's being friendless as a recommendation; dejection, and incapacity of struggling through the world, as a motive for assisting him; in a word, to consider these circumstances of disadvantage, which are usually thought a sufficient reason for neglect and overlooking a person, as a motive for helping him forward: this is the course of benevolence which compassion marks out and directs us to: this is that humanity which is so peculiarly becoming our nature and circumstances in this world.

To these considerations, drawn from the nature of man, must be added the reason of the thing itself we are recommending, which accords to and shows the same. For since it is so much more in our power to lessen the misery of our fellow-creatures than to promote their positive happiness; in cases where there is an inconsistency, we shall be likely to do much more good by setting ourselves to mitigate the former than by endeavouring to promote the latter. Let the competition be between the poor and the rich. It is easy, you will say, to see which will have the preference. True; but the question is, which ought to to have the preference? What proportion is there between the happiness produced by doing a favour to the indigent, and that produced by doing the same favour to one in easy circumstances? It is manifest that the addition of a very large estate to one who before had an affluence, will in many instances yield him less new enjoyment or satisfaction than an ordinary charity would yield to a necessitous person. So that it is not only true that our nature, *i.e.*, the voice of God within us, carries us to the exercise of charity and benevolence in the way of compassion or mercy, preferably to any other way; but we also manifestly discern much more good done by the former; or, if you will allow me the expressions, more misery annihilated and happiness created. If charity and benevolence, and endeavouring to do good to our fellow-creatures, be anything, this observation deserves to be most seriously considered by all who have to bestow. And it holds with great exactness, when applied to the several degrees of greater and less indigency throughout the various ranks in human life: the happiness or good produced not being in proportion to what is bestowed, but in proportion to this joined with the need there was of it.

It may perhaps be expected that upon this subject notice should be taken of occasions, circumstances, and characters which seem at once to call forth affections of different sorts. Thus vice may be thought the object both of pity and indignation: folly, of pity and of laughter. How far this is strictly true, I shall not inquire; but only observe upon the appearance, how much more humane it is to yield and give scope to affections, which are most directly in favour of, and friendly towards, our fellow-creatures; and that there is plainly much less danger of being led wrong by these than by the other.

But, notwithstanding all that has been said in recommendation of compassion, that it is most amiable, most becoming human nature, and most useful to the world; yet it must be owned that every affection, as distinct from a principle of reason, may rise too high, and be beyond its just proportion. And by means of this one carried too far, a man throughout his life is subject to much more uneasiness than belongs to his share; and in particular instances, it may be in such a degree as to incapacitate him from assisting the very person who is the object of it. But as there are some who upon principle set up for suppressing this affection itself as weakness, there is also I know not what of fashion on this side; and, by some means or other, the whole world almost is run into the extremes of insensibility towards the distresses of their fellow-creatures: so that general rules and exhortations must always be on the other side.

And now to go on to the uses we should make of the foregoing reflections, the further ones they lead to, and the general temper they have a tendency to beget in us.

There being that distinct affection implanted in the nature of man, tending to lessen the miseries of life, that particular provision made for abating its sorrows, more than for increasing its positive happiness, as before explained; this may suggest to us what should be our general aim respecting ourselves, in our passage through this world: namely, to endeavour chiefly to escape misery, keep free from uneasiness, pain, and sorrow, or to get relief and mitigation of them; to propose to ourselves peace and tranquillity of mind, rather than pursue after high enjoyments. This is what the constitution of nature before explained marks out as the course we should follow, and the end we should aim at. To make pleasure and mirth and jollity our business, and be constantly hurrying about after some gay amusement, some new gratification of sense or appetite, to those who will consider the nature of man and our condition in this world, will appear the most romantic scheme of life that ever entered into thought. And yet how many are there who go on in this course, without learning better from the daily, the hourly disappointments, listlessness, and satiety which accompany this fashionable method of wasting away their days!

The subject we have been insisting upon would lead us into the same kind of reflections by a different connection. The miseries of life brought home to ourselves by compassion, viewed through this affection considered as the sense by which they are perceived, would beget in us that moderation, humility, and soberness of mind which has been now recommended; and which peculiarly belongs to a season of recollection, the only purpose of which is to bring us to a just sense of things, to recover us out of that forgetfulness of ourselves, and our true state, which it is manifest far the greatest part of men pass their whole life in. Upon this account Solomon says that *it is better to go to the house of mourning than to go to the house of feasting;* i.e., it is more to a man's advantage to turn his eyes towards objects of distress, to recall sometimes to his remembrance the occasions of sorrow, than to pass all his days in thoughtless mirth and gaiety. And he represents the wise as choosing to frequent the former of these places; to be sure not for his own sake, but because *by the sadness of the countenance, the heart is made b. t'er.* Every one observes how temperate and reasonable men are when humbled and brought low by afflictions in comparison of what they are in high prosperity. By this voluntary resort to the house of mourning, which is here recommended, we might learn all those useful instructions which calamities teach without undergoing them ourselves; and grow wiser and better at a more easy rate than men commonly do. The objects themselves, which in that place of sorrow lie before our view, naturally give us a seriousness and attention, check that wantonness which is the growth of prosperity and ease, and lead us to reflect upon the deficiencies of human life itself; that *every man at his best estate is altogether vanity.* This would correct the florid and gaudy prospects and expectations which we are too apt to indulge, teach us to lower our notions of happiness and enjoyment, bring them down to the reality of things, to what is attainable, to what the frailty of our condition will admit of, which, for any continuance, is only tranquillity, ease, and moderate satisfactions. Thus we might at once become proof against the temptations with which the whole world almost is carried away; since it is plain that not only what is called a life of pleasure, but also vicious pursuits in general, aim at somewhat besides and beyond these moderate satisfactions.

And as to that obstinacy and wilfulness, which renders men so insensible to the motives of religion; this right sense of ourselves and of the world about us would bend the stubborn mind, soften the heart, and make it more apt to receive impression; and this is the proper temper in which to call our ways to remembrance, to review and set home upon ourselves the miscarriages of our past life. In such a compliant state of mind, reason and conscience will have a fair hearing; which is the preparation for, or rather the beginning of, that repentance, the outward show of which we all put on at this season.

Lastly, The various miseries of life which lie before

us wherever we turn our eyes, the frailty of this mortal state we are passing through, may put us in mind that the present world is not our home; that we are merely strangers and travellers in it, as all our fathers were. It is therefore to be considered as a foreign country; in which our poverty and wants, and the insufficient supplies of them, were designed to turn our views to that higher and better state we are heirs to: a state where will be no follies to be overlooked, no miseries to be pitied, no wants to be relieved; where the affection we have been now treating of will happily be lost, as there will be no objects to exercise it upon: for *God shall wipe away all tears from their eyes, and there shall be no more death, neither sorrow, nor crying; neither shall there be any more pain; for the former things are passed away.*

SERMON VII.

UPON THE CHARACTER OF BALAAM.
PREACHED THE SECOND SUNDAY AFTER EASTER.

NUMBERS xxiii. 10.

Let me die the death of the righteous, and let my last end be like his.

THESE words, taken alone, and without respect to him who spoke them, lead our thoughts immediately to the different ends of good and bad men. For though the comparison is not expressed, yet it is manifestly implied; as is also the preference of one of these characters to the other in that last circumstance, death. And, since dying the death of the righteous or of the wicked necessarily implies men's being righteous or wicked; *i.e.*, having lived righteously or wickedly; a comparison of them in their lives also might come into consideration, from such a single view of the words themselves. But my present design is to consider them with a particular reference or respect to him who spoke them; which reference, if you please to attend, you will see. And if what shall be offered to your consideration at this time be thought a discourse upon the whole history of this man, rather than upon the particular words I have read, this is of no consequence: it is sufficient if it afford reflection of use and service to ourselves.

But, in order to avoid cavils respecting this remarkable relation in Scripture, either that part of it which you have heard in the first lesson for the day, or any other; let me just observe that as this is not a place for answering them, so they no way affect the following discourse; since the character there given is plainly a real one in life, and such as there are parallels to.

The occasion of Balaam's coming out of his own country into the land of Moab, where he pronounced this solemn prayer or wish, he himself relates in the first parable or prophetic speech, of which it is the conclusion. In which is a custom referred to, proper to be taken notice of: that of devoting enemies to destruction before the entrance upon a war with them. This custom appears to have prevailed over a great part of the world; for we find it amongst the most distant nations. The Romans had public officers, to whom it belonged as a stated part of their office. But there was somewhat more particular in the case now before us: Balaam being looked upon as an extraordinary person, whose blessing or curse was thought to be always effectual.

In order to engage the reader's attention to this passage, the sacred historian has enumerated the preparatory circumstances, which are these. Balaam requires the king of Moab to build him seven altars, and to prepare him the same number of oxen and of rams. The sacrifice being over, he retires alone to a solitude sacred to these occasions, there to wait the Divine inspiration or answer, for which the foregoing rites were the preparation. *And God met Balaam, and put a word in his mouth;* * upon receiving which, he returns back to the altars, where was the king, who had all this while attended the sacrifice, as appointed; he and all the princes of Moab standing, big with expectation of the Prophet's reply. *And he took up his parable, and said, Balak the king of Moab hath brought me from Aram, out of the mountains of the east, saying, Come, curse me Jacob, and come, defy Israel. How shall I curse, whom God hath not cursed? Or how shall I defy, whom the Lord hath not defied? For from the top of the rocks I see him, and from the hills I behold him: lo, the people shall dwell alone, and shall not be reckoned among the nations. Who can count the dust of Jacob, and the number of the fourth part of Israel? Let me die the death of the righteous, and let my last end be like his.*†

It is necessary, as you will see in the progress of this discourse, particularly to observe what he understood by *righteous*. And he himself is introduced in the book of Micah ‡ explaining it; if by *righteous* is meant *good*, as to be sure it is. *O my people, remember now what Balak king of Moab consulted, and*

---

* Ver. 4, 5. † Ver. 6. ‡ Micah vi.

what Balaam the son of Beor answered him from Shittim unto Gilgal. From the mention of Shittim it is manifest that it is this very story which is here referred to, though another part of it, the account of which is not now extant; as there are many quotations in Scripture out of books which are not come down to us. *Remember what Balaam answered, that ye may know the righteousness of the Lord;* i.e., the righteousness which God will accept. Balak demands, *Wherewith shall I come before the Lord, and bow myself before the high God? Shall I come before him with burnt-offerings, with calves of a year old? Will the Lord be pleased with thousands of rams, or with ten thousands of rivers of oil? Shall I give my first-born for my transgression, the fruit of my body for the sin of my soul?* Balaam answers him, *He hath showed thee, O man, what is good: and what doth the Lord require of thee, but to do justly, and to love mercy, and to walk humbly with thy God?* Here is a good man expressly characterised, as distinct from a dishonest and a superstitious man. No words can more strongly exclude dishonesty and falseness of heart than *doing justice and loving mercy;* and both these, as well as *walking humbly with God,* are put in opposition to those ceremonial methods of recommendation, which Balak hoped might have served the turn. From hence appears what he meant by the *righteous,* whose *death* he desires to die.

Whether it was his own character shall now be inquired; and in order to determine it, we must take a view of his whole behaviour upon this occasion. When the elders of Moab came to him, though he appears to have been much allured with the rewards offered, yet he had such regard to the authority of God as to keep the messengers in suspense until he had consulted His will. *And God said to him, Thou shalt not go with them; thou shalt not curse the people, for they are blessed.** Upon this he dismisses the ambassadors, with an absolute refusal of accompanying them back to their king. Thus far his regards to his duty prevailed, neither does there anything appear as yet amiss in his conduct. His answer being reported to the king of Moab, a more honourable embassy is immediately despatched, and greater rewards proposed. Then the iniquity of his heart began to disclose itself. A thorough honest man would without hesitation have repeated his former answer, that he could not be guilty of so infamous a prostitution of the sacred character with which he was invested, as in the name of a prophet to curse those whom he knew to be blessed. But instead of this, which was the only honest part in these circumstances that lay before him, he desires the princes of Moab to tarry that night with him also; and for the sake of the reward deliberates, whether by some means or other he might not be able to obtain leave to

* Chap. xxii. 12.

curse Israel; to do that, which had been before revealed to him to be contrary to the will of God, which yet he resolves not to do without that permission. Upon which, as when this nation afterwards rejected God from reigning over them, He gave them a king in His anger; in the same way, as appears from other parts of the narration, He gives Balaam the permission he desired: for this is the most natural sense of the words. Arriving in the territories of Moab, and being received with particular distinction by the king, and he repeating in person the promise of the rewards he had before made to him by his ambassadors, he seeks, the text says, by *sacrifices* and *enchantments* (what these were is not to our purpose), to obtain leave of God to curse the people; keeping still his resolution, not to do it without that permission: which not being able to obtain, he had such regard to the command of God as to keep this resolution to the last. The supposition of his being under a supernatural restraint is a mere fiction of Philo: he is plainly represented to be under no other force or restraint than the fear of God. However, he goes on persevering in that endeavour, after he had declared that *God had not beheld iniquity in Jacob, neither had he seen perverseness in Israel;** *i.e.*, they were a people of virtue and piety, so far as not to have drawn down by their iniquity that curse which he was soliciting leave to pronounce upon them. So that the state of

* Ver. 21.

Balaam's mind was this: he wanted to do what he knew to be very wicked, and contrary to the express command of God; he had inward checks and restraints which he could not entirely get over; he therefore casts about for ways to reconcile this wickedness with his duty. How great a paradox soever this may appear, as it is indeed a contradiction in terms, it is the very account which the Scripture gives us of him.

But there is a more surprising piece of iniquity yet behind. Not daring in his religious character, as a prophet, to assist the king of Moab, he considers whether there might not be found some other means of assisting him against that very people, whom he himself by the fear of God was restrained from cursing in words. One would not think it possible that the weakness, even of religious self-deceit in its utmost excess, could have so poor a distinction, so fond an evasion, to serve itself of. But so it was; and he could think of no other method than to betray the children of Israel to provoke His wrath, who was their only strength and defence. The temptation which he pitched upon was that concerning which Solomon afterwards observed, that it had *cast down many wounded; yea, many strong men had been slain by it:* and of which he himself was a sad example, when *his wives turned away his heart after other gods.* This succeeded: the people sin against God; and thus the Prophet's counsel brought on that destruction which he could by no means be prevailed upon to assist with the religious ceremony of execration, which the king of Moab thought would itself have affected it. Their crime and punishment are related in Deuteronomy * and Numbers.† And from the relation repeated in Numbers,‡ it appears, that Balaam was the contriver of the whole matter. It is also ascribed to him in the Revelation, § where he is said to have *taught Balak to cast a stumbling-block before the children of Israel.*

This was the man, this Balaam, I say, was the man, who desired to *die the death of the righteous,* and that his *last end might be like his;* and this was the state of his mind when he pronounced these words.

So that the object we have now before us is the most astonishing in the world: a very wicked man, under a deep sense of God and religion, persisting still in his wickedness, and preferring the wages of unrighteousness, even when he had before him a lively view of death, and that approaching period of his days, which should deprive him of all those advantages for which he was prostituting himself; and likewise a prospect, whether certain or uncertain, of a future state of retribution; all this joined with an explicit ardent wish that, when he was to leave this world, he might be in the condition of a righteous man. Good God! what inconsistency, what perplexity is here! With what

* Chap. iv.   † Chap. xxv.
‡ Chap. xxxi.   § Chap. ii.

different views of things, with what contradictory principles of action, must such a mind be torn and distracted! It was not unthinking carelessness, by which he ran on headlong in vice and folly, without ever making a stand to ask himself what he was doing: no; he acted upon the cool motives of interest and advantage. Neither was he totally hard and callous to impressions of religion, what we call abandoned; for he absolutely denied to curse Israel. When reason assumes her place, when convinced of his duty, when he owns and feels, and is actually under the influence of the divine authority; whilst he is carrying on his views to the grave, the end of all temporal greatness; under this sense of things, with the better character and more desirable state present—full before him—in his thoughts, in his wishes, voluntarily to choose the worse—what fatality is here! Or how otherwise can such a character be explained? And yet, strange as it may appear, it is not altogether an uncommon one: nay, with some small alterations, and put a little lower, it is applicable to a very considerable part of the world. For if the reasonable choice be seen and acknowledged, and yet men make the unreasonable one, is not this the same contradiction; that very inconsistency, which appeared so unaccountable?

To give some little opening to such characters and behaviour, it is to be observed in general that there is no account to be given in the way of reason, of men's so strong attachments to the present world: our hopes and fears and pursuits are in degrees beyond all proportion to the known value of the things they respect. This may be said without taking into consideration religion and a future state; and when these are considered, the disproportion is infinitely heightened. Now when men go against their reason, and contradict a more important interest at a distance, for one nearer, though of less consideration; if this be the whole of the case, all that can be said is, that strong passions, some kind of brute force within, prevails over the principle of rationality. However, if this be with a clear, full, and distinct view of the truth of things, then it is doing the utmost violence to themselves, acting in the most palpable contradiction to their very nature. But if there be any such thing in mankind as putting half-deceits upon themselves; which there plainly is, either by avoiding reflection, or (if they do reflect) by religious equivocation, subterfuges, and palliating matters to themselves; by these means conscience may be laid asleep, and they may go on in a course of wickedness with less disturbance. All the various turns, doubles, and intricacies in a dishonest heart cannot be unfolded or laid open; but that there is somewhat of that kind is manifest, be it to be called self-deceit, or by any other name. Balaam had before his eyes the authority of God, absolutely forbidding him what he, for the sake of a reward, had the strongest inclination to : he was likewise in a state of mind sober enough to consider death and his last end: by these considerations he was restrained, first from going to the king of Moab, and after he did go, from cursing Israel. But notwithstanding this, there was great wickedness in his heart. He could not forego the rewards of unrighteousness : he therefore first seeks for indulgences, and when these could not be obtained, he sins against the whole meaning, end, and design of the prohibition, which no consideration in the world could prevail with him to go against the letter of. And surely that impious counsel he gave to Balak against the children of Israel was, considered in itself, a greater piece of wickedness than if he had cursed them in words.

If it be inquired what his situation, his hopes, and fears were, in respect to this his wish; the answer must be, that consciousness of the wickedness of his heart must necessarily have destroyed all settled hopes of dying the death of the righteous: he could have no calm satisfaction in this view of his last end : yet, on the other hand, it is possible that those partial regards to his duty, now mentioned, might keep him from perfect despair.

Upon the whole it is manifest that Balaam had the most just and true notions of God and religion; as appears, partly from the original story itself, and more plainly from the passage in Micah; where he explains religion to consist in real virtue and real piety, expressly distinguished from superstition, and in terms which most strongly exclude dishonesty and falseness of heart. Yet you see his behaviour: he seeks indulgences for plain wickedness, which not being able to obtain he glosses over that same wickedness, dresses it up in a new form, in order to make it pass off more easily with himself. That is, he deliberately contrives to deceive and impose upon himself in a matter which he knew to be of the utmost importance.

To bring these observations home to ourselves: it is too evident that many persons allow themselves in very unjustifiable courses who yet make great pretences to religion; not to deceive the world, none can be so weak as to think this will pass in our age; but from principles, hopes, and fears, respecting God and a future state; and go on thus with a sort of tranquillity and quiet of mind. This cannot be upon a thorough consideration, and full resolution, that the pleasures and advantages they propose are to be pursued at all hazards, against reason, against the law of God, and though everlasting destruction is to be the consequence. This would be doing too great violence upon themselves. No, they are for making a composition with the Almighty. These of His commands they will obey; but as to others—why, they will make all the atonements in their power; the ambitious, the covetous, the dissolute man, each in a way which shall not contradict his respective pursuit. Indulgences before, which was Balaam's first attempt, though he was not so successful in it as to deceive himself, or atonements afterwards, are all the same. And here, perhaps, come in faint hopes that they may, and half-resolves that they will, one time or other, make a change.

Besides these there are also persons, who, from a more just way of considering things, see the infinite absurdity of this, of substituting sacrifice instead of obedience; there are persons far enough from superstition, and not without some real sense of God and religion upon their minds; who yet are guilty of most unjustifiable practices, and go on with great coolness and command over themselves. The same dishonesty and unsoundness of heart discovers itself in these another way. In all common ordinary cases we see intuitively at first view what is our duty, what is the honest part. This is the ground of the observation, that the first thought is often the best. In these cases doubt and deliberation is itself dishonesty, as it was in Balaam upon the second message. That which is called considering what is our duty in a particular case is very often nothing but endeavouring to explain it away. Thus those courses, which, if men would fairly attend to the dictates of their own consciences, they would see to be corruption, excess, oppression, uncharitableness; these are refined upon—things were so and so circumstantiated—great difficulties are raised about fixing bounds and degrees, and thus every moral obligation whatever may be evaded. Here is scope, I say, for an unfair mind to explain away every moral obligation to itself. Whether men reflect again upon this internal management and artifice, and how explicit they are with themselves, is another question. There are many operations of the mind, many things pass within, which we never reflect upon again; which a bystander, from having frequent opportunities of observing us and our conduct, may make shrewd guesses at.

That great numbers are in this way of deceiving themselves is certain. There is scarce a man in the world, who has entirely got over all regards, hopes, and fears, concerning God and a future state; and these apprehensions in the generality, bad as we are, prevail in considerable degrees: yet men will and can be wicked, with calmness and thought; we see they are. There must therefore be some method of making it sit a little easy upon their minds; which, in the superstitious, is those indulgences and atonements before mentioned, and this self-deceit of another kind in persons of another character. And both these proceed from a certain unfairness of mind, a peculiar inward dishonesty; the direct contrary to that simplicity which our Saviour recommends, under the notion of *becoming little children*, as a necessary qualification for our entering into the kingdom of heaven.

But to conclude: How much soever men differ in the course of life they prefer, and in their ways of palliating and excusing their vices to themselves; yet all agree in one thing, desiring to *die the death of the righteous*. This is surely remarkable. The observation may be extended further, and put thus: even without determining what that is which we call guilt or innocence, there is no man but would choose, after having had the pleasure or advantage of a vicious action, to be free of the guilt of it, to be in the state of an innocent man. This shows at least the disturbance and implicit dissatisfaction in vice. If we inquire into the grounds of it, we shall find it proceeds partly from an immediate sense of having done evil, and partly from an apprehension that this inward sense shall one time or another be seconded by a higher judgment, upon which our whole being depends. Now to suspend and drown this sense, and these apprehensions, be it by the hurry of business or of pleasure, or by superstition, or moral equivocations, this is in a manner one and the same, and makes no alteration at all in the nature of our case. Things and actions are what they are, and the consequences of them will be what they will be: why, then, should we desire to be deceived? As we are reasonable creatures, and have any regard to ourselves, we ought to lay these things plainly and honestly before our mind, and upon this, act as you please, as you think most fit: make that choice, and prefer that course of life, which you can justify to yourselves, and which sits most easy upon your own mind. It will immediately appear that vice cannot be the happiness, but must upon the whole be the misery, of such a creature as man; a moral, an accountable agent. Superstitious observances, self-deceit though of a more refined sort, will not in reality at all mend matters with us. And the result of the whole can be nothing else, but that with simplicity and fairness we *keep innocency, and take heed unto the thing that is right: for this alone shall bring a man peace at the last.*

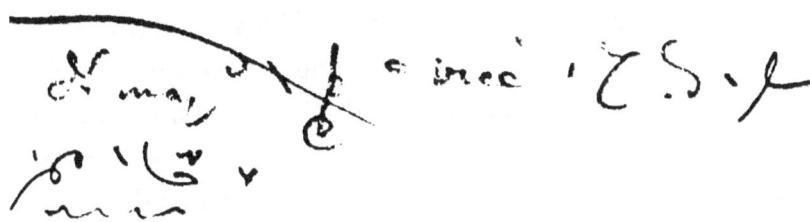

SERMON XI.

UPON THE LOVE OF OUR NEIGHBOUR.
PREACHED ON ADVENT SUNDAY.

ROMANS xiii. 9.

And if there be any other commandment, it is briefly comprehended in this saying, namely, Thou shalt love thy neighbour as thyself.

It is commonly observed that there is a disposition in men to complain of the viciousness and corruption of the age in which they live as greater than that of former ones; which is usually followed with this further observation, that mankind has been in that respect much the same in all times. Now, not to determine whether this last be not contradicted by the accounts of history; thus much can scarce be doubted, that vice and folly takes different turns, and some particular kinds of it are more open and avowed in some ages than in others; and, I suppose, it may be spoken of as very much the distinction of the present to profess a contracted spirit, and greater regards to self-interest, than appears to have been done formerly. Upon this account it seems worth while to inquire whether private interest is likely to be promoted in proportion to the degree in which self-love engrosses us, and prevails over all other principles; *or whether the contracted affection may not possibly be so prevalent as to disappoint itself, and even contradict its own and private good.*

And since, further, there is generally thought to be some peculiar kind of contrariety between self-love and the love of our neighbour, between the pursuit of public and of private good; insomuch that when you are recommending one of these, you are supposed to be speaking against the other; and from hence arises a secret prejudice against, and frequently open scorn of, all talk of public spirit and real good-will to our fellow-creatures; it will be necessary to *inquire what respect benevolence hath to self-love, and the pursuit of private interest to the pursuit of public:* or whether there be anything of that peculiar inconsistence and contrariety between them over and above what there is between self-love and other passions and particular affections, and their respective pursuits.

These inquiries, it is hoped, may be favourably attended to; for there shall be all possible concessions made to the favourite passion, which hath so much allowed to it, and whose cause is so universally pleaded: it shall be treated with the utmost tenderness and concern for its interests.

In order to do this, as well as to determine the fore-mentioned questions, it will be necessary to *consider the nature, the object, and end of that self-love, as distinguished from other principles or affections in the mind, and their respective objects.*

Every man hath a general desire of his own happiness; and likewise a variety of particular affections, passions, and appetites to particular external objects. The former proceeds from, or is, self-love; and seems inseparable from all sensible creatures, who can reflect upon themselves and their own interest or happiness so as to have that interest an object to their minds; what is to be said of the latter is, that they proceed from or together make up that particular nature, according to which man is made. The object the former pursues is somewhat internal—our own happiness, enjoyment, satisfaction; whether we have, or have not, a distinct particular perception what it is, or wherein it consists: the objects of the latter are this or that particular external thing, which the affections tend towards, and of which it hath always a particular idea or perception. The principle we call self-love never seeks anything external for the sake of the thing, but only as a means of happiness or good: particular affections rest in the external things themselves. One belongs to man as a reasonable creature reflecting upon his own interest or happiness. The other, though quite distinct from reason, are as much a part of human nature.

That all particular appetites and passions are towards *external things themselves*, distinct from the *pleasure arising from them*, is manifested from hence;

that there could not be this pleasure, were it not for that prior suitableness between the object and the passion: there could be no enjoyment or delight from one thing more than another, from eating food more than from swallowing a stone, if there were not an affection or appetite to one thing more than another.

Every particular affection, even the love of our neighbour, is as really our own affection as self-love; and the pleasure arising from its gratification is as much my own pleasure as the pleasure self-love would have from knowing I myself should be happy some time hence would be my own pleasure. And if, because every particular affection is a man's own, and the pleasure arising from its gratification his own pleasure, or pleasure to himself, such particular affection must be called self-love; according to this way of speaking, no creature whatever can possibly act but merely from self-love; and every action and every affection whatever is to be resolved up into this one principle. But then this is not the language of mankind; or if it were, we should want words to express the difference between the principle of an action, proceeding from cool consideration that it will be to my own advantage; and an action, suppose of revenge or of friendship, by which a man runs upon certain ruin, to do evil or good to another. It is manifest the principles of these actions are totally different, and so want different words to be distinguished by; all that they agree in is that they both proceed from, and are done to gratify, an inclination in a man's self. But the principle or inclination in one case is self-love; in the other, hatred or love of another. There is then a distinction between the cool principle of self-love, or general desire of our own happiness, as one part of our nature, and one principle of action; and the particular affections towards particular external objects, as another part of our nature, and another principle of action. How much soever therefore is to be allowed to self-love, yet it cannot be allowed to be the whole of our inward constitution; because, you see, there are other parts or principles which come into it.

Further, private happiness or good is all which self-love can make us desire, or be concerned about: in having this consists its gratification: it is an affection to ourselves; a regard to our own interest, happiness, and private good: and in the proportion a man hath this, he is interested, or a lover of himself. Let this be kept in mind; because there is commonly, as I shall presently have occasion to observe, another sense put upon these words. On the other hand, particular affections tend towards particular external things: these are their objects: having these is their end: in this consists their gratification: no matter whether it be, or be not, upon the whole, our interest or happiness. An action done from the former of these principles is called an interested action. An action proceeding from any of the latter has its denomination of passionate, ambitious, friendly, revengeful, or any other, from the particular appetite or affection from which it proceeds. Thus self-love as one part of human nature, and the several particular principles as the other part, are, themselves, their objects and ends, stated and shown.

From hence it will be easy to see how far, and in what ways, each of these can contribute and be subservient to the private good of the individual. Happiness does not consist in self-love. The desire of happiness is no more the thing itself than the desire of riches is the possession or enjoyment of them. People might love themselves with the most entire and unbounded affection, and yet be extremely miserable. Neither can self-love any way help them out, but by setting them on work to get rid of the causes of their misery, to gain or make use of those objects which are by nature adapted to afford satisfaction. Happiness or satisfaction consists only in the enjoyment of those objects which are by nature suited to our several particular appetites, passions, and affections. So that if self-love wholly engrosses us, and leaves no room for any other principle, there can be absolutely no such thing at all as happiness or enjoyment of any kind whatever; since happiness consists in the gratification of particular passions, which supposes the having of them. Self-love then does not constitute *this* or *that* to be our interest or good; but, our interest or good being constituted by nature and supposed, self-love only puts us upon obtaining and securing it. Therefore, if it be possible that self-love may prevail and exert itself in a degree or manner which is not subservient to this end; then it will not follow that our interest will be promoted in proportion to the degree in which that principle engrosses us, and prevails over others. Nay, further, the private and contracted affection, when it is not subservient to this end, private good may, for anything that appears, have a direct contrary tendency and effect. And if we will consider the matter, we shall see that it often really has. *Disengagement* is absolutely necessary to enjoyment; and a person may have so steady and fixed an eye upon his own interest, whatever he places it in, as may hinder him from *attending* to many gratifications within his reach, which others have their minds *free* and *open* to. Over-fondness for a child is not generally thought to be for its advantage; and, if there be any guess to be made from appearances, surely that character we call selfish is not the most promising for happiness. Such a temper may plainly be, and exert itself in a degree and manner which may give unnecessary and useless solicitude and anxiety, in a degree and manner which may prevent obtaining the means and materials of enjoyment, as well as the making use of them. Immoderate self-love does very ill consult its own interest: and, how much soever a paradox it may appear, it is certainly true that even from self-love we should endeavour to get over all inordinate regard to and consideration of ourselves. Every one of our passions and affections hath its natural stint and bound, which may easily be exceeded; whereas our enjoyments can possibly be but in a determinate measure and degree. Therefore such excess of the affection, since it cannot procure any enjoyment, must in all cases be useless; but is generally attended with inconveniences, and often is downright pain and misery. This holds as much with regard to self-love as to all other affections. The natural degree of it, so far as it sets us on work to gain and make use of the materials of satisfaction, may be to our real advantage; but beyond or besides this, it is in several respects an inconvenience and disadvantage. Thus it appears that private interest is so far from being likely to be promoted in proportion to the degree in which self-love engrosses us, and prevails over all other principles, that *the contracted affection may be so prevalent as to disappoint itself, and even contradict its own and private good.*

"But who, except the most sordidly covetous, ever thought there was any rivalship between the love of greatness, honour, power, or between sensual appetites and self-love? No, there is a perfect harmony between them. It is by means of these particular appetites and affections that self-love is gratified in enjoyment, happiness, and satisfaction. The competition and rivalship is between self-love and the love of our neighbour: that affection which leads us out of ourselves, makes us regardless of our own interest, and substitute that of another in its stead." Whether, then, there be any peculiar competition and contrariety in this case shall now be considered.

Self-love and interestedness was stated to consist in or be an affection to ourselves, a regard to our own private good: it is therefore distinct from benevolence, which is an affection to the good of our fellow-creatures. But that benevolence is distinct from, that is, not the same thing with self-love, is no reason for its being looked upon with any peculiar suspicion; because every principle whatever, by means of which self-love is gratified, is distinct from it; and all things which are distinct from each other are equally so. A man has an affection or aversion to another: that one of these tends to, and is gratified by, doing good, that the other tends to, and is gratified by, doing harm, does not in the least alter the respect which either one or the other of these inward feelings has to self-love. We use the word *property* so as to exclude any other persons having an interest in that of which we say a particular man has the property. And we often use the word *selfish* so as to exclude in the same manner all regards to the good of others. But the cases are not parallel: for though that exclusion is really part of the idea of property; yet such positive exclusion, or bringing this peculiar disregard to the good of others into the idea of self-love, is in reality adding to the idea, or changing it from what it was before stated to consist in, namely, in an affection to ourselves.* This being the whole idea of self-love, it can no otherwise exclude good-will or love of others, than merely by not including it, no otherwise, than it excludes love of arts or reputation, or of anything else. Neither on the other hand does benevolence, any more than love of arts or of reputation exclude self-love. Love of our neighbour, then, has just the same respect to, is no more distant from, self-love, than hatred of our neighbour, or than love or hatred of anything else. Thus the principles, from which men rush upon certain ruin for the destruction of an enemy, and for the preservation of a friend, have the same respect to the private affection, and are equally interested, or equally disinterested; and it is of no avail whether they are said to be one or the other. Therefore to those who are shocked to hear virtue spoken of as disinterested, it may be allowed that it is indeed absurd to speak thus of it; unless hatred, several

* P. 137.

particular instances of vice, and all the common affections and aversions in mankind, are acknowledged to be disinterested too. Is there any less inconsistence between the love of inanimate things, or of creatures merely sensitive, and self-love, than between self-love and the love of our neighbour? Is desire of and delight in the happiness of another any more a diminution of self-love than desire of and delight in the esteem of another? They are both equally desire of and delight in somewhat external to ourselves; either both or neither are so. The object of self-love is expressed in the term self; and every appetite of sense, and every particular affection of the heart, are equally interested or disinterested, because the objects of them all are equally self or somewhat else. Whatever ridicule therefore the mention of a disinterested principle or action may be supposed to lie open to, must, upon the matter being thus stated, relate to ambition, and every appetite and particular affection as much as to benevolence. And indeed all the ridicule, and all the grave perplexity, of which this subject hath had its full share, is merely from words. The most intelligible way of speaking of it seems to be this: that self-love and the actions done in consequence of it (for these will presently appear to be the same as to this question) are interested; that particular affections towards external objects, and the actions done in consequence of those affections are not so. But every one is at liberty to use words as he pleases. All that is here insisted upon is that ambition, revenge, benevolence, all particular passions whatever, and the actions they produce, are equally interested or disinterested.

Thus it appears that there is no peculiar contrariety between self-love and benevolence; no greater competition between these than between any other particular affections and self-love. This relates to the affections themselves. Let us now see whether there be any peculiar contrariety between the respective courses of life which these affections lead to; whether there be any greater competition between the pursuit of private and of public good, than between any other particular pursuits and that of private good.

There seems no other reason to suspect that there is any such peculiar contrariety, but only that the course of action which benevolence leads to has a more direct tendency to promote the good of others, than that course of action which love of reputation suppose, or any other particular affection leads to. But that any affection tends to the happiness of another does not hinder its tending to one's own happiness too. That others enjoy the benefit of the air and the light of the sun does not hinder but that these are as much one's own private advantage now as they would be if we had the property of them exclusive of all others. So a pursuit which tends to promote the good of another, yet may have as great tendency to promote private interest, as a pursuit which does not tend to the good of another at all, or which is mischievous to him. All particular affections whatever, resentment, benevolence, love of arts, equally lead to a course of action for their own gratification; *i.e.*, the gratification of ourselves; and the gratification of each gives delight: so far, then, it is manifest they have all the same respect to private interest. Now take into consideration, further, concerning these three pursuits, that the end of the first is the harm, of the second, the good of another, of the last, somewhat indifferent; and is there any necessity that these additional considerations should alter the respect, which we before saw these three pursuits had to private interest, or render any one of them less conducive to it, than any other? Thus one man's affection is to honour as his end; in order to obtain which he thinks no pains too great. Suppose another, with such a singularity of mind, as to have the same affection to public good as his end, which he endeavours with the same labour to obtain. In case of success, surely the man of benevolence hath as great enjoyment as the man of ambition; they both equally having the end their affections, in the same degree, tended to; but in case of disappointment, the benevolent man has clearly the advantage; since endeavouring to do good, considered as a virtuous pursuit, is gratified by its own consciousness, *i.e.*, is in a degree its own reward.

And as to these two, or benevolence and any other particular passions whatever, considered in a further view, as forming a general temper, which more or less disposes us for enjoyment of all the common blessings of life, distinct from their own gratification, is benevolence less the temper of tranquillity and freedom than ambition or covetousness? Does the benevolent man appear less easy with himself from his love to his neighbour? Does he less relish his being? Is there any peculiar gloom seated on his face? Is his mind less open to entertainment, to any particular gratification? Nothing is more manifest than that being in good humour, which is benevolence whilst it lasts, is itself the temper of satisfaction and enjoyment.

Suppose then, a man sitting down to consider how he might become most easy to himself, and attain the greatest pleasure he could, all that which is his real natural happiness. This can only consist in the enjoyment of those objects which are by nature adapted to our several faculties. These particular enjoyments make up the sum total of our happiness, and they are supposed to arise from riches, honours, and the gratification of sensual appetites. Be it so; yet none profess themselves so completely happy in these enjoyments but that there is room left in the mind for others, if they were presented to them: nay, these, as much as they engage us, are not thought so high. but that human nature is capable even of greater. Now there have been persons in all ages who have professed that they found satisfaction in the exercise of charity, in the love of their neighbour, in endeavouring to promote the happiness of all they had to do with, and in the pursuit of what is just and right and good as the general bent of their mind and end of their life; and that doing an action of baseness or cruelty would be as great violence to *their* self, as much breaking in upon their nature, as any external force. Persons of this character would add, if they might be heard, that they consider themselves as acting in the view of an Infinite Being, who is in a much higher sense the object of reverence and of love, than all the world besides; and therefore they could have no more enjoyment from a wicked action done under His eye than the persons to whom they are making their apology could if all mankind were the spectators of it; and that the satisfaction of approving themselves to his unerring judgment, to whom they thus refer all their actions, is a more continued settled satisfaction than any this world can afford; as also that they have, no less than others, a mind free and open to all the common innocent gratifications of it, such as they are. And if we go no further, does there appear any absurdity in this? Will any one take upon him to say that a man cannot find his account in this general course of life as much as in the most unbounded ambition, and the excesses of pleasure? Or that such a person has not consulted so well for himself, for the satisfaction and peace of his own mind, as the ambitious or dissolute man? And though the consideration that God himself will in the end justify their taste, and support their cause, is not formally to be insisted upon here, yet thus much comes in, that all enjoyments whatever are much more clear and unmixed from the assurance that they will end well. Is it certain, then, that there is nothing in these pretensions to happiness? especially when there are not wanting persons who have supported themselves with satisfactions of this kind in sickness, poverty, disgrace, and in the very pangs of death; whereas it is manifest all other enjoyments fail in these circumstances. This surely looks suspicious of having somewhat in it. Self-love, methinks, should be alarmed. May she not possibly pass over greater pleasures than those she is so wholly taken up with?

The short of the matter is no more than this. Happiness consists in the gratification of certain affections, appetites, passions, with objects which are by nature adapted to them. Self-love may indeed set us on work to gratify these, but happiness or enjoyment has no immediate connection with self-love, but arises from such gratification alone. Love of our neighbour is one of those affections. This, considered as a *virtuous principle*, is gratified by a consciousness of *endeavouring* to promote the good of others, but considered as a natural affection, its gratification consists in the actual accomplishment of this endeavour. Now indulgence or gratification of this affection, whether in that consciousness or this accomplishment, has the same respect to interest as indulgence of any other affection; they equally proceed from or do not proceed from self-love, they equally include or equally exclude this principle. Thus it appears, that *benevolence and the pursuit of public good hath at least as great respect to self-love and the pursuit of private good as any other particular passions, and their respective pursuits.*

Neither is covetousness, whether as a temper or pursuit, any exception to this. For if by covetousness is meant the desire and pursuit of riches for their own sake, without any regard to, or consideration of, the uses of them, this hath as little to do with self-love as benevolence hath. But by this word is usually meant, not such madness and total distraction of mind, but immoderate affection to and pursuit of riches as possessions in order to some further end, namely, satisfaction, interest, or good. This, therefore, is not a particular affection or particular pursuit, but it is the general principle of self-love, and the general pursuit of our own interest, for which reason the word *selfish* is by every one appropriated to this temper and pursuit. Now as it is ridiculous to assert that self-love and the love of our neighbour are the same, so neither is it asserted that following these different affections hath the same tendency and respect to our own interest. The comparison is not between self-love and the love of our neighbour, between pursuit of our own interest and the interest of others, but between the several particular affections in human nature towards external objects, as one part of the comparison, and the one particular affection to the good of our neighbour as the other part of it: and it has been shown that all these have the same respect to self-love and private interest.

There is indeed frequently an inconsistence or interfering between self-love or private interest and the several particular appetites, passions, affections, or the pursuits they lead to. But this competition or interfering is merely accidental, and happens much oftener between pride, revenge, sensual gratifications, and private interest, than between private interest and benevolence. For nothing is more common than to see men give themselves up to a passion or an affection to their known prejudice and ruin, and in direct contradiction to manifest and real interest, and the loudest calls of self-love: whereas the seeming competitions and interfering, between benevolence and private interest, relate much more to the materials or means of enjoyment than to enjoyment itself. There is often an interfering in the former when there is none in the latter. Thus as to riches: so much money as a man gives away, so much less will remain in his possession.—Here is a real interfering. But though a man cannot possibly give without lessening his fortune, yet there are multitudes might give without lessening their own enjoyment, because they may have more than they can turn to any real use or advantage to themselves. Thus the more thought and time any one employs about the interests and good of others, he must necessarily have less to attend his own: but he may have so ready and large a supply of his own wants, that such thought might be really useless to himself, though of great service and assistance to others.

The general mistake, that there is some greater inconsistence between endeavouring to promote the good of another and self-interest, than between self-interest and pursuing anything else, seems, as hath already been hinted, to arise from our notions of property, and to be carried on by this property's being supposed to be itself our happiness or good. People are so very much taken up with this one subject, that they seem from it to have formed a general way of thinking, which they apply to other things that they have nothing to do with. Hence in a confused and slight way it might well be taken for granted that another's having no interest in an affection (*i.e.*, his good not being the object of it) renders, as one may speak, the proprietor's interest in it greater; and that if another had an interest in it this would render his less, or occasion that such affection could not be so friendly to self-love, or conducive to private good, as an affection or pursuit which has not a regard to the good of another. This, I say, might be taken for granted, whilst it was not attended to, that the object of every particular affection is equally somewhat external to ourselves, and whether it be the good of another person, or whether it be any other external thing, makes no alteration with regard to its being one's own affection, and the gratification of it one's own private enjoyment. And so far as it is taken for granted that barely having the means and materials of enjoyment is what constitutes interest and happiness; that our interest or good consists in possessions themselves, in having the property of riches, houses, lands, gardens, not in the enjoyment of them; so far it will even more strongly be taken for granted, in the way already explained, that an affection's conducing to the good of another must even necessarily occasion it to conduce less to private good, if not to be positively detrimental to it. For, if property and happiness are one and the same thing, as by increasing the property of another you lessen your own property, so by promoting the happiness of another you must lessen your own happiness. But whatever occasioned the mistake,

I hope it has been fully proved to be one, as it has been proved, that there is no peculiar rivalship or competition between self-love and benevolence: that as there may be a competition between these two, so there may also between any particular affection whatever and self-love; that every particular affection, benevolence among the rest, is subservient to self-love by being the instrument of private enjoyment; and that in one respect benevolence contributes more to private interest, *i.e.*, enjoyment or satisfaction, than any other of the particular common affections, as it is in a degree its own gratification.

And to all these things may be added that religion, from whence arises our strongest obligation to benevolence, is so far from disowning the principle of self-love, that it often addresses itself to that very principle, and always to the mind in that state when reason presides, and there can no access be had to the understanding, but by convincing men that the course of life we would persuade them to is not contrary to their <u>interest</u>. It may be allowed, without any prejudice to the cause of virtue and religion, that our ideas of happiness and misery are of all our ideas the nearest and most important to us; that they will, nay, if you please, that they ought to prevail over those of order, and beauty, and harmony, and proportion, if there should ever be, as it is impossible there ever should be, any inconsistence between them, though these last, too, as expressing the fitness of actions, are real as truth itself. Let it be allowed, though virtue or moral rectitude does indeed consist in affection to and pursuit of what is right and good, as such, yet, that when we sit down in a cool hour, we can neither justify to ourselves this or any other pursuit, till we are convinced that it will be for our happiness, or at least not contrary to it.

Common reason and humanity will have some influence upon mankind, whatever becomes of speculations; but, so far as the interests of virtue depend upon the theory of it being secured from open scorn, so far its very being in the world depends upon its appearing to have no contrariety to private interest and self-love. The foregoing observations, therefore, it is hoped, may have gained a little ground in favour of the precept before us, the particular explanation of which shall be the subject of the next discourse.

I will conclude at present with observing the peculiar obligation which we are under to virtue and religion, as enforced in the verses following the text, in the epistle for the day, from our Saviour's coming into the world. *The night is far spent, the day is at hand; let us therefore cast off the works of darkness, and let us put on the armour of light,* &c. The meaning and force of which exhortation is, that Christianity lays us under new obligations to a good life, as by it the will of God is more clearly revealed, and as it affords additional motives to the practice of it, over and above those which arise out of the nature of virtue and vice, I might add, as our Saviour has set us a perfect example of goodness in our own nature. Now love and charity is plainly the thing in which He hath placed His religion; in which, therefore, as we have any pretence to the name of Christians, we must place ours. He hath at once enjoined it upon us by way of command with peculiar force, and by His example, as having undertaken the work of our salvation out of pure love and goodwill to mankind. The endeavour to set home this example upon our minds is a very proper employment of this season, which is bringing on the festival of His birth, which, as it may teach us many excellent lessons of humility, resignation, and obedience to the will of God, so there is none it recommends with greater authority, force, and advantage than this love and charity, since it was *for us men, and for our salvation*, that *He came down from heaven, and was incarnate, and was made man*, that He might teach us our duty, and more especially that He might enforce the practice of it, reform mankind, and finally bring us to that *eternal salvation*, of which *He is the Author to all those that obey Him*.

SERMON XII.

UPON THE LOVE OF OUR NEIGHBOUR.

Rom. xiii. 9.

And if there be any other commandment, it is briefly comprehended in this saying, namely, Thou shalt love thy neighbour as thyself.

HAVING already removed the prejudices against public spirit, or the love of our neighbour, on the side of private interest and self-love, I proceed to the particular explanation of the precept before us, by showing, *Who is our neighbour : In what sense we are required to love him as ourselves; The influence such love would have upon our behaviour in life; and lastly, How this commandment comprehends in it all others.*

I. The objects and due extent of this affection will be understood by attending to the nature of it, and to the nature and circumstances of mankind in this world. The love of our neighbour is the same with charity, benevolence, or goodwill: it is an affection to the good and happiness of our fellow-creatures. This implies in it a disposition to produce happiness, and this is the simple notion of goodness, which appears so amiable wherever we meet with it. From hence it is easy to see that the perfection of goodness consists in love to the whole universe. This is the perfection of Almighty God.

But as man is so much limited in his capacity, as so small a part of the Creation comes under his notice and influence, and as we are not used to consider things in so general a way, it is not to be thought of that the universe should be the object of benevolence to such creatures as we are. Thus in that precept of our Saviour, *Be ye perfect, even as your Father, which is in heaven, is perfect,** the perfection of the divine goodness is proposed to our imitation as it is promiscuous, and extends to the evil as well as the good; not as it is absolutely universal, imitation of it in this respect being plainly beyond us. The object is too vast. For this reason moral writers also have substituted a less general object for our benevolence, mankind. But this likewise is an object too general, and very much out of our view. Therefore persons more practical have, instead of mankind, put our country, and made the principle of virtue, of human virtue, to consist in the entire uniform love of our country: and this is what we call a public spirit, which in men of public stations is the character of a patriot. But this is speaking to the upper part of the world. Kingdoms and governments are large, and the sphere of action of far the greatest part of mankind is much narrower than the government they live under: or however,

* Matt. v. 48.

common men do not consider their actions as affecting the whole community of which they are members. There plainly is wanting a less general and nearer object of benevolence for the bulk of men than that of their country. Therefore the Scripture, not being a book of theory and speculation, but a plain rule of life for mankind, has with the utmost possible propriety put the principle of virtue upon the love of our neighbour, which is that part of the universe, that part of mankind, that part of our country, which comes under our immediate notice, acquaintance, and influence, and with which we have to do.

This is plainly the true account or reason why our Saviour places the principle of virtue in the love of our *neighbour*, and the account itself shows who are comprehended under that relation.

II. Let us now consider in what sense we are commanded to love our neighbour *as ourselves*.

This precept, in its first delivery by our Saviour, is thus introduced:—*Thou shalt love the Lord thy God with all thine heart, with all thy soul, and with all thy strength; and thy neighbour as thyself.* These very different manners of expression do not lead our thoughts to the same measure or degree of love, common to both objects, but to one peculiar to each. Supposing, then, which is to be supposed, a distinct meaning and propriety in the words, *as thyself;* the precept we are considering will admit of any of these senses: that we bear the *same kind* of affection to our neighbour as we do to ourselves, or, that the love we bear to our neighbour should have *some certain proportion or other* to self-love: or, lastly, that it should bear the particular proportion of *equality*, that *it be in the same degree.*

First, The precept may be understood as requiring only that we have the *same kind* of affection to our fellow-creatures as to ourselves; that, as every man has the principle of self-love, which disposes him to avoid misery, and consult his own happiness, so we should cultivate the affection of goodwill to our neighbour, and that it should influence us to have the same kind of regard to him. This at least must be commanded, and this will not only prevent our being injurious to him, but will also put us upon promoting his good. There are blessings in life, which we share in common with others, peace, plenty, freedom, healthful seasons. But real benevolence to our fellow-creatures would give us the notion of a common interest in a stricter sense, for in the degree we love another, his interest, his joys and sorrows, are our own. It is from self-love that we form the notion of private good, and consider it is our own: love of our neighbour would teach us thus to appropriate to ourselves his good and welfare; to consider ourselves as having a real share in his happiness. Thus the principle of benevolence would be an advocate within our own breasts, to take care of the interests of our fellow-creatures in all the interfering and competitions which cannot but be, from the imperfection of our nature, and the state we are in. It would likewise, in some measure, lessen that interfering, and hinder men from forming so strong a notion of private good, exclusive of the good of others, as we commonly do. Thus, as the private affection makes us in a peculiar manner sensible of humanity, justice or injustice, when exercised towards ourselves, love of our neighbour would give us the same kind of sensibility in his behalf. This would be the greatest security of our uniform obedience to that most equitable rule. *Whatsoever ye would that men should do unto you, do ye even so unto them.*

All this is indeed no more than that we should have a real love to our neighbour; but then, which is to be observed, the words *as thyself* express this in the most distinct manner, and determine the precept to relate to the affection itself. The advantage which this principle of benevolence has over other remote considerations is, that it is itself the temper of virtue, and likewise that it is the chief, nay, the only effectual security of our performing the several offices of kindness we owe to our fellow-creatures. When from distant considerations men resolve upon any thing to which they have no liking, or perhaps an averseness, they are perpetually finding out evasions and excuses, which need never be wanting, if people look for them: and they equivocate with themselves in the plainest cases in the world. This may be in respect to single determinate acts of virtue, but it comes in much more, where the obligation is to a general course of behaviour, and most of all, if it be such as cannot be reduced to fixed determinate rules. This observation may account for the diversity of the expression in that known passage of the prophet Micah, *to do justly, and to love mercy.* A man's heart must be formed to humanity and benevolence, he must *love mercy,* otherwise he will not act mercifully in any settled course of behaviour. As consideration of the future sanctions of religion is our only security of preserving in our duty, in cases of great temptation: so to get our heart and temper formed to a love and liking of what is good is absolutely necessary in order to our behaving rightly in the familiar and daily intercourses amongst mankind.

Secondly, The precept before us may be understood to require that we love our neighbour in some certain *proportion* or other, *according as* we love ourselves. And indeed a man's character cannot be determined by the love he bears to his neighbour, considered absolutely, but the proportion which this bears to self-love, whether it be attended to or not, is the chief thing which forms the character and influences the actions. For, as the form of the body is a composition of various parts, so likewise our inward structure is not simple or uniform, but a composition of various passions, appetites, affections, together with rationality, including in this last both the discernment of what is right, and a disposition to regulate ourselves by it. There is greater variety of parts in what we call a character than there are features in a face, and the morality of that is no more determined by one part than the beauty or deformity of this is by one single feature: each is to be judged of by all the parts or features, not taken singly, but together. In the inward frame the various passions, appetites, affections, stand in different respects to each other. The principles in our mind may be contradictory, or checks and allays only, or incentives and assistants to each other. And principles, which in their nature have no kind of contrariety or affinity, may yet accidentally be each other's allays or incentives.

From hence it comes to pass, that though we were able to look into the inward contexture of the heart, and see with the greatest exactness in what degree any one principle is in a particular man, we could not from thence determine how far that principle would go towards forming the character, or what influence it would have upon the actions, unless we could likewise discern what other principles prevailed in him, and see the proportion which that one bears to the others. Thus, though two men should have the affection of compassion in the same degree exactly, yet one may have the principle of resentment or of ambition so strong in him as to prevail over that of compassion, and prevent its having any influence upon his actions, so that he may deserve the character of a hard or cruel man, whereas the other having compassion in just the same degree only, yet having resentment or ambition in a lower degree, his compassion may prevail over them, so as to influence his actions, and to denominate his temper compassionate. So that, how strange soever it may appear to people who do not attend to the thing, yet it is quite manifest that, when we say one man is more resenting or compassionate than another, this does not necessarily imply that one has the principle of resentment or of compassion stronger than the other. For if the proportion which resentment or compassion bears to other inward principles is greater in one than in the other, this is itself sufficient to denominate one more resenting or compassionate than the other.

Further, the whole system, as I may speak, of affections (including rationality), which constitute the heart, as this word is used in Scripture and on moral subjects, are each and all of them stronger in some than in others. Now the proportion which the two general affections, benevolence and self-love, bear to each other, according to this interpretation of the text, denominates men's character as to virtue. Suppose, then, one man to have the principle of benevolence in a higher degree than another; it will not follow from hence that his general temper or character or actions will be more benevolent than the other's. For he may have self-love in such a degree as quite to prevail over benevolence, so that it may have no influence at all upon his action, whereas benevolence in the other person, though in a lower degree, may yet be the strongest principle in his heart, and strong enough to be the guide of his actions, so as to denominate him a good and virtuous man. The case is here as in scales: it is not one weight considered in itself, which determines whether the scale shall ascend or descend, but this depends upon the proportion which that one weight hath to the other.

It being thus manifest that the influence which benevolence has upon our actions, and how far it goes towards forming our character, is not determined by the degree itself of this principle in our mind, but by the proportion it has to self-love and other principles: a comparison also being made in the text between self-love and the love of our neighbour; these joint considerations afforded sufficient occasion for treating here of that proportion. It plainly is implied in the precept, though it should be questioned, whether it be the exact meaning of the words, as *thyself*.

Love of our neighbour, then, must bear some proportion to self-love, and virtue, to be sure, consists in the due proportion. What this due proportion is, whether as a principle in the mind, or as exerted in actions, can be judged of only from our nature and condition in this world. Of the degree in which affections and the principles of action, considered in themselves, prevail, we have no measure: let us, then, proceed to the course of behaviour, the actions they produce.

Both our nature and condition require that each particular man should make particular provision for himself: and the inquiry, what proportion benevolence should have to self-love, when brought down to practice, will be, what is a competent care and provision for ourselves? And how certain soever it be that each man must determine this for himself, and how ridiculous soever it would be for any to attempt to determine it for another, yet it is to be observed that the proportion is real, and that a competent provision has a bound, and that it cannot be all which we can possibly get and keep within our grasp, without legal injustice. Mankind almost universally bring in vanity, supplies for what is called a life of pleasure, covetousness, or imaginary notions of superiority over others, to determine this question: but every one who desires to act a proper part in society would do well to consider how far any of them come in to determine it, in the way of moral consideration. All that can be said is, supposing what, as the world goes, is so much to be supposed that it is scarce to be mentioned, that persons do not neglect what they really owe to themselves; the more of their care and thought and of their fortune they employ in doing good to their fellow-creatures the nearer they come up to the law of perfection, *Thou shalt love thy neighbour as thyself.*

Thirdly, if the words *as thyself* were to be understood of an equality of affection, it would not be attended with those consequences which perhaps may be thought to follow from it. Suppose a person to have the same settled regard to others as to himself; that in every deliberate scheme or pursuit he took their interest into the account in the same degree as his own, so far as an equality of affection would produce this: yet he would, in fact, and ought to be, much more taken up and employed about himself, and his own concerns, than about others, and their interests. For, besides the one common affection toward himself and his neighbour he would have several other particular affections, passions, appetites, which he could not possibly feel in common both for himself and others. Now these sensations themselves very much employ us, and have perhaps as great influence as self-love. So far indeed as self-love, and cool reflection upon what is for our interest, would set us on work to gain a supply of our own several wants, so far the love of our neighbour would make us do the same for him: but the degree in which we are put upon seeking and making use of the means of gratification, by the feeling of those affections, appetites, and passions, must necessarily be peculiar to ourselves.

That there are particular passions (suppose shame, resentment) which men seem to have, and feel in common, both for themselves and others, makes no alteration in respect to those passions and appetites which cannot possibly be thus felt in common. From hence (and perhaps more things of the like kind might be mentioned) it follows, that though there were an equality of affection to both, yet regards to ourselves would be more prevalent than attention to the concerns of others.

And from moral considerations it ought to be so, supposing still the equality of affection commanded, because we are in a peculiar manner, as I may speak, intrusted with ourselves, and therefore care of our own interests, as well as of our conduct, particularly belongs to us.

To these things must be added, that moral obligations can extend no further than to natural possibilities. Now we have a perception of our own interests, like consciousness of our own existence, which we always carry about with us, and which, in its continuation, kind, and degree, seems impossible to be felt in respect to the interests of others.

From all these things it fully appears that though we were to love our neighbour in the same degree as we love ourselves, so far as this is possible, yet the care of ourselves, of the individual, would not be neglected, the apprehended danger of which seems to be the only objection against understanding the precept in this strict sense.

III. The general temper of mind which the due love of our neighbour would form us to, and the influence it would have upon our behaviour in life, is now to be considered.

The temper and behaviour of charity is explained at large in that known passage of St. Paul:* *Charity suffereth long, and is kind; charity envieth not, doth not behave itself unseemly, seeketh not her own, thinketh no evil, beareth all things, believeth all things, hopeth all things.* As to the meaning of the expressions, *seeketh not her own, thinketh no evil, believeth all things;* however those expressions may be explained away, this meekness, and in some degree easiness of temper, readiness to forego our right for the sake of peace, as well as in the way of compassion, freedom from mistrust,

* I Cor. xiii.

and disposition to believe well of our neighbour, this general temper, I say, accompanies, and is plainly the effect of love and goodwill. And, though such is the world in which we live, that experience and knowledge of it not only may, but must beget, in us greater regard to ourselves, and doubtfulness of the characters of others, than is natural to mankind, yet these ought not to be carried further than the nature and course of things make necessary. It is still true, even in the present state of things, bad as it is, that a real good man had rather be deceived than be suspicious; had rather forego his known right, than run the venture of doing even a hard thing. This is the general temper of that charity, of which the apostle asserts, that if he had it not, giving his *body to be burned would avail him nothing;* and which he says *shall never fail.*

The happy influence of this temper extends to every different relation and circumstance in human life. It plainly renders a man better, more to be desired, as to all the respects and relations we can stand in to each other. The benevolent man is disposed to make use of all external advantages in such a manner as shall contribute to the good of others, as well as to his own satisfaction. His own satisfaction consists in this. He will be easy and kind to his dependents, compassionate to the poor and distressed, friendly to all with whom he has to do.

This includes the good neighbour, parent, master. magistrate: and such a behaviour would plainly make dependence, inferiority, and even servitude, easy. So that a good or charitable man of superior rank in wisdom, fortune, authority, is a common blessing to the place he lives in: happiness grows under his influence. This good principle in inferiors would discover itself in paying respect, gratitude, obedience, as due. It were therefore, methinks, one just way of trying one's own character to ask ourselves, am I in reality a better master or servant, a better friend, a better neighbour, than such and such persons, whom, perhaps, I may think not to deserve the character of virtue and religion so much as myself?

And as to the spirit of party, which unhappily prevails amongst mankind, whatever are the distinctions which serve for a supply to it, some or other of which have obtained in all ages and countries, one who is thus friendly to his kind will immediately make due allowances for it, as what cannot but be amongst such creatures as men, in such a world as this. And as wrath and fury and overbearing upon these occasions proceed, as I may speak, from men's feeling only on their own side, so a common feeling, for others as well as for ourselves, would render us sensible to this truth, which it is strange can have so little influence, that we ourselves differ from others, just as much as they do from us. I put the matter in this way, because it can scarce be expected that the generality of men should see that those things which are made the occasions of dissension and fomenting the party-spirit are really nothing at all: but it may be expected from all people, how much soever they are in earnest about their respective peculiarities, that humanity and common goodwill to their fellow-creatures should moderate and restrain that wretched spirit.

This good temper of charity likewise would prevent strife and enmity arising from other occasions: it would prevent our giving just cause of offence, and our taking it without cause. And in cases of real injury, a good man will make all the allowances which are to be made, and, without any attempts of retaliation, he will only consult his own and other men's security for the future against injustice and wrong.

IV. I proceed to consider, lastly, what is affirmed of the precept now explained, that it comprehends in it all others, *i.e.*, that to love our neighbour as ourselves includes in it all virtues.

Now the way in which every maxim of conduct, or general speculative assertion, when it is to be explained at large should be treated, is, to show what are the particular truths which were designed to be comprehended under such a general observation.

how far it is strictly true, and then the limitations, restrictions, and exceptions, if there be exceptions, with which it is to be understood. But it is only the former of these, namely, how far the assertion in the text holds, and the ground of the pre-eminence assigned to the precept of it, which in strictness comes into our present consideration.

However, in almost everything that is said, there is somewhat to be understood beyond what is explicitly laid down, and which we of course supply, somewhat, I mean, which would not be commonly called a restriction or limitation. Thus, when benevolence is said to be the sum of virtue, it is not spoken of as a blind propension, but as a principle in reasonable creatures, and so to be directed by their reason, for reason and reflection comes into our notion of a moral agent. And that will lead us to consider distant consequences, as well as the immediate tendency of an action. It will teach us that the care of some persons, suppose children and families, is particularly committed to our charge by Nature and Providence, as also that there are other circumstances, suppose friendship or former obligations, which require that we do good to some, preferably to others. Reason, considered merely as subservient to benevolence, as assisting to produce the greatest good, will teach us to have particular regard to these relations and circumstances, because it is plainly for the good of the world that they should be regarded. And as there are numberless cases in which, notwithstanding appearances, we are not competent judges, whether a particular action will upon the whole do good or harm, reason in the same way will teach us to be cautious how we act in these cases of uncertainty. It will suggest to our consideration which is the safer side; how liable we are to be led wrong by passion and private interest; and what regard is due to laws, and the judgment of mankind. All these things must come into consideration, were it only in order to determine which way of acting is likely to produce the greatest good. Thus, upon supposition that it were in the strictest sense true, without limitation, that benevolence includes in it all virtues, yet reason must come in as its guide and director, in order to attain its own end, the end of benevolence, the greatest public good. Reason, then, being thus included, let us now consider the truth of the assertion itself.

First, It is manifest that nothing can be of consequence to mankind or any creature but happiness. This, then, is all which any person can, in strictness of speaking, be said to have a right to. We can therefore *owe no man anything*, but only to further and promote his happiness, according to our abilities. And therefore a disposition and endeavour to do good to all with whom we have to do, in the degree and manner which the different relations we stand in to them require, is a discharge of all the obligations we are under to them.

As human nature is not one simple uniform thing, but a composition of various parts, body, spirit, appetites, particular passions, and affections, for each of which reasonable self-love would lead men to have due regard, and make suitable provision, so society consists of various parts to which we stand in different respects and relations, and just benevolence would as surely lead us to have due regard to each of these, and behave as the respective relations require. Reasonable goodwill and right behaviour towards our fellow-creatures are in a manner the same, only that the former expresseth the principle as it is in the mind; the latter, the principle as it were become external, *i.e.*, exerted in actions.

And so far as temperance, sobriety, and moderation in sensual pleasures, and the contrary vices, have any respect to our fellow-creatures, any influence upon their quiet, welfare, and happiness, as they always have a real, and often a near influence upon it, so far it is manifest those virtues may be produced by the love of our neighbour, and that the contrary vices would be prevented by it. Indeed, if men's regard to themselves will not restrain them from excess, it may be thought little probable that their love to others will be sufficient: but the reason is, that their love to others is not, any more than their regard to themselves, just, and in its due degree. There are, however, manifest instances of persons kept sober and temperate from regard to their affairs, and the welfare of those who depend upon them. And it is obvious to every one that habitual excess, a dissolute course of life, implies a general neglect of the duties we owe towards our friends, our families, and our country.

From hence it is manifest that the common virtues and the common vices of mankind may be traced up to benevolence, or the want of it. And this entitles the precept, *Thou shalt love thy neighbour as thyself*, to the pre-eminence given to it, and is a justification of the apostle's assertion, that all other commandments are comprehended in it, whatever cautions and restrictions * there are, which might require to be

---

* For instance: as we are not competent judges, what is upon the whole for the good of the world, there may be other immediate ends appointed us to pursue, besides that one of doing good or producing happiness. Though the good of the Creation be the only end of the Author of it, yet he may have laid us under particular obligations, which we may discern and feel ourselves under, quite distinct from a perception, that the observance or violation of them it for the happiness or misery of our fellow-creatures. And this is in fact the case, for there are certain dispositions of mind, and certain actions, which are in themselves approved or disapproved by mankind, abstracted from the consideration of their tendency to the happiness or misery of the world; approved or disapproved by reflection, by that principle within, which is the guide of life, the judge of right and wrong. Numberless instances of this kind might be mentioned. There are pieces of treachery, which in themselves appear base and detestable

considered, if we were to state particularly and at length what is virtue and and right behaviour in mankind. But,

Secondly, It might be added, that in a higher and more general way of consideration, leaving out the particular nature of creatures, and the particular circumstances in which they are placed, benevolence seems in the strictest sense to include in it all that is good and worthy, all that is good, which we have any distinct particular notion of. We have no clear conception of any position moral attribute in the Supreme Being, but what may be resolved up into goodness. And, if we consider a reasonable creature or moral agent, without regard to the particular relations and circumstances in which he is placed, we cannot

---

to every one. There are actions, which perhaps can scarce have any other general name given them than indecencies, which yet are odious and shocking to human nature. There is such a thing as meanness, a little mind, which as it is quite distinct from incapacity, so it raises a dislike and disapprobation quite different from that contempt, which men are too apt to have, of mere folly. On the other hand, what we call greatness of mind is the object of another sort of approbation, than superior understanding. Fidelity, honour, strict justice, are themselves approved in the highest degree, abstracted from the consideration of their tendency. Now, whether it be thought that each of these are connected with benevolence in our nature, and so may be considered as the same thing with it, or whether some of them be thought an inferior kind of virtues and vices, somewhat like natural beauties and deformities, or lastly, plain exceptions to the general rule, thus much however is certain, that the things now instanced in, and numberless others, are approved or disapproved by mankind in general, in quite another view than as conducive to the happiness or misery of the World

conceive anything else to come in towards determining whether he is to be ranked in a higher or lower class of virtuous beings, but the higher or lower degree in which that principle, and what is manifestly connected with it, prevail in him.

That which we more strictly call piety, or the love of God, and which is an essential part of a right temper, some may perhaps imagine no way connected with benevolence: yet surely they must be connected, if there be indeed in being an object infinitely good. Human nature is so constituted that every good affection implies the love of itself, *i.e.*, becomes the object of a new affection in the same person. Thus, to be righteous, implies in it the love of righteousness; to be benevolent, the love of benevolence; to be good, the love of goodness; whether this righteousness, benevolence, or goodness be viewed as in our own mind or another's, and the love of God as a being perfectly good is the love of perfect goodness contemplated in a being or person. Thus morality and religion, virtue and piety, will at last necessarily coincide, run up into one and the same point, and *love* will be in all senses *the end of the commandment.*

> *O Almighty God, inspire us with this divine principle; kill in us all the seeds of envy and ill-will; and help us, by cultivating within ourselves the love of our neighbour, to improve in the love of*

Thee. Thou hast placed us in various kindreds, friendships, and relations, as the school of discipline for our affections: help us, by the due exercise of them, to improve to perfection; till all partial affection be lost in that entire universal one, and thou, O *God, shalt* be all in all.

SERMON XIII., XIV.

UPON THE LOVE OF GOD.

MATTHEW xxii. 37.

Thou shalt love the Lord thy God with all thy heart, and with all thy soul, and with all thy mind.

EVERYBODY knows, you therefore need only just be put in mind, that there is such a thing as having so great horror of one extreme as to run insensibly and of course into the contrary; and that a doctrine's having been a shelter for enthusiasm, or made to serve the purposes of superstition, is no proof of the falsity of it: truth or right being somewhat real in itself, and so not to be judged of by its liableness to abuse, or by its supposed distance from or nearness to error. It may be sufficient to have mentioned this in general, without taking notice of the particular extravagances which have been vented under the pretence or endeavour of explaining the love of God; or how manifestly we are got into the contrary extreme, under the notion of a reasonable religion; so very reasonable as to have nothing to do with the heart and affections, if these words signify anything but the faculty by which we discern speculative truth.

By the love of God I would understand all those

regards, all those affections of mind which are due immediately to Him from such a creature as man, and which rest in Him as their end. As this does not include servile fear, so neither will any other regards, how reasonable soever, which respect anything out of or besides the perfection of the Divine nature, come into consideration here. But all fear is not excluded, because His displeasure is itself the natural proper object of fear. Reverence, ambition of His love and approbation, delight in the hope or consciousness of it, come likewise into this definition of the love of God, because He is the natural object of all those affections or movements of mind as really as He is the object of the affection, which is in the strictest sense called love; and all of them equally rest in Him as their end. And they may all be understood to be implied in these words of our Saviour, without putting any force upon them: for He is speaking of the love of God and our neighbour as containing the whole of piety and virtue.

It is plain that the nature of man is so constituted as to feel certain affections upon the sight or contemplation of certain objects. Now the very notion of affection implies resting in its object as an end. And the particular affection to good characters, reverence and moral love of them, is natural to all those who have any degree of real goodness in themselves. This will be illustrated by the description of a perfect character in a creature; and by considering the manner in which a good man in his presence would be affected towards such a character. He would of course feel the affections of love, reverence, desire of his approbation, delight in the hope or consciousness of it. And surely all this is applicable, and may be brought up to that Being, who is infinitely more than an adequate object of all those affections; whom we are commanded to *love with all our heart, with all our soul, and with all our mind.* And of these regards towards Almighty God some are more particularly suitable to and becoming so imperfect a creature as man, in this mortal state we are passing through; and some of them, and perhaps other exercises of the mind, will be the employment and happiness of good men in a state of perfection.

This is a general view of what the following discourse will contain. And it is manifest the subject is a real one: there is nothing in it enthusiastical or unreasonable. And if it be indeed at all a subject, it is one of the utmost importance.

As mankind have a faculty by which they discern speculative truth, so we have various affections towards external objects. Understanding and temper, reason and affection, are as distinct ideas as reason and hunger, and one would think could no more be confounded. It is by reason that we get the ideas of several objects of our affections; but in these cases reason and affection are no more the same than sight of a particular object, and the pleasure or uneasiness consequent thereupon, are the same. Now as reason tends to and rests in the discernment of truth, the object of it, so the very nature of affection consists in tending towards, and resting in, its objects as an end. We do indeed often in common language say that things are loved, desired, esteemed, not for themselves, but for somewhat further, somewhat out of and beyond them; yet, in these cases, whoever will attend will see that these things are not in reality the objects of the affections, *i.e.* are not loved, desired, esteemed, but the somewhat further and beyond them. If we have no affections which rest in what are called their objects, then what is called affection, love, desire, hope, in human nature, is only an uneasiness in being at rest; an unquiet disposition to action, progress, pursuit, without end or meaning. But if there be any such thing as delight in the company of one person, rather than of another; whether in the way of friendship, or mirth and entertainment, it is all one, if it be without respect to fortune, honour, or increasing our stores of knowledge, or anything beyond the present time; here is an instance of an affection absolutely resting in its object as its end, and being gratified in the same way as the appetite of hunger is satisfied with food. Yet nothing is more common than to hear it asked, what advantage a man hath in such a course, suppose of study, particular friendships, or in any other; nothing, I say, is more common than to hear such a question put in a way which supposes no gain, advantage, or interest, but as a means to somewhat further: and if so, then there is no such thing at all as real interest, gain, or advantage. This is the same absurdity with respect to life as an infinite series of effects without a cause is in speculation. The gain, advantage, or interest consists in the delight itself, arising from such a faculty's having its object: neither is there any such thing as happiness or enjoyment but what arises from hence. The pleasures of hope and of reflection are not exceptions: the former being only this happiness anticipated; the latter the same happiness enjoyed over again after its time. And even the general expectation of future happiness can afford satisfaction only as it is a present object to the principle of self-love.

It was doubtless intended that life should be very much a pursuit to the gross of mankind. But this is carried so much further than is reasonable that what gives immediate satisfaction, *i.e.* our present interest, is scarce considered as our interest at all. It is inventions which have only a remote tendency towards enjoyment, perhaps but a remote tendency towards gaining the means only of enjoyment, which are chiefly spoken of as useful to the world. And though his way of thinking were just with respect to the imperfect state we are now in, where we know so little of satisfaction without satiety, yet it must be guarded against when we are considering the happiness of a state of perfection; which happiness being enjoyment and not hope, must necessarily consist in this, that our affections have their objects, and rest in those objects as an end, *i.e.* be satisfied with them. This will further appear in the sequel of this discourse.

Of the several affections, or inward sensations, which particular objects excite in man, there are some, the having of which implies the love of them, when they are reflected upon.* This cannot be said of all our affections, principles, and motives of action. It were ridiculous to assert that a man upon reflection hath the same kind of approbation of the appetite of hunger or the passion of fear as he hath of goodwill to his fellow-creatures. To be a just, a good, a righteous man, plainly carries with it a peculiar affection to or love of justice, goodness, righteousness, when these principles are the objects of contemplation. Now if a man approves of, or hath an affection to, any principle in and for itself, incidental things allowed

---

* St. Austin observes, Amor ipse ordinate amandus est, quo bene amatur quod amandum est, ut sit in nobis virtus qua vivitur bene, i e. *The affection which we rightly have for what is lovely must ordinate justly, in due manner and proportion, become the object of a new affection, or be itself beloved, in order to our being endued with that virtue which is the principle of a good life.* Civ. Dei, l. xv. c. 22.

for, it will be the same whether he views it in his own mind or in another; in himself or in his neighbour. This is the account of our approbation of, or moral love and affection to good characters; which cannot but be in those who have any degrees of real goodness in themselves, and who discern and take notice of the same principle in others.

From observation of what passes within ourselves, our own actions, and the behaviour of others, the mind may carry on its reflections as far as it pleases; much beyond what we experience in ourselves, or discern in our fellow creatures. It may go on and consider goodness as become a uniform continued principle of action, as conducted by reason, and forming a temper and character absolutely good and perfect, which is in a higher sense excellent, and proportionably the object of love and approbation.

Let us then suppose a creature perfect according to his created nature—let his form be human, and his capacities no more than equal to those of the chief of men—goodness shall be his proper character, with wisdom to direct it, and power within some certain determined sphere of action to exert it: but goodness must be the simple actuating principle within him; this being the moral quality which is amiable, or the immediate object of love as distinct from other affections of approbation. Here then is a finite object for our mind to tend towards, to exercise itself upon: a creature, perfect according to his capacity, fixed, steady, equally unmoved by weak pity or more weak fury and resentment; forming the justest scheme of conduct; going on undisturbed in the execution of it, through the several methods of severity and reward, towards his end, namely, the general happiness of all with whom he hath to do, as in itself right and valuable. This character, though uniform in itself, in its principle, yet exerting itself in different ways, or considered in different views, may by its appearing variety move different affections. Thus, the severity of justice would not affect us in the same way as an act of mercy. The adventitious qualities of wisdom and power may be considered in themselves; and even the strength of mind which this immovable goodness supposes may likewise be viewed as an object of contemplation distinct from the goodness itself. Superior excellence of any kind, as well as superior wisdom and power, is the object of awe and reverence to all creatures, whatever their moral character be; but so far as creatures of the lowest rank were good, so far the view of this character, as simply good, must appear amiable to them, be the object of, or beget love. Further suppose we were conscious that this superior person so far approved of us that we had nothing servilely to fear from him; that he was really our friend, and kind and good to us in particular, as he had occasionally intercourse with us: we must be other creatures than we are, or we could not but feel the same kind of satisfaction and enjoyment (whatever would be the degree of it) from this higher acquaintance and friendship as we feel from common ones, the intercourse being real and the persons equally present in both cases. We should have a more ardent desire to be approved by his better judgment, and a satisfaction in that approbation of the same sort with what would be felt in respect to common persons, or be wrought in us by their presence.

Let us now raise the character, and suppose this creature, for we are still going on with the supposition of a creature, our proper guardian and governor; that we were in a progress of being towards somewhat further; and that his scheme of government was too vast for our capacities to comprehend: remembering still that he is perfectly good, and our friend as well as our governor. Wisdom, power, goodness, accidentally viewed anywhere, would inspire reverence, awe, love; and as these affections would be raised in higher or lower degrees in proportion as we had occasionally more or less intercourse with the creature endued with those qualities, so this further consideration and knowledge that he was our proper guardian and governor would much more bring these objects and qualities home to ourselves; teach us they had a greater respect to us in particular, that we had a higher interest in that wisdom and power and goodness. We should, with joy, gratitude, reverence, love, trust, and dependence, appropriate the character, as what we had a right in, and make our boast in such our relation to it. And the conclusion of the whole would be that we should refer ourselves implicitly to him, and cast ourselves entirely upon him. As the whole attention of life should be to obey his commands, so the highest enjoyment of it must arise from the contemplation of this character, and our relation to it, from a consciousness of his favour and approbation, and from the exercise of those affections towards him which could not but be raised from his presence. A Being who hath these attributes, who stands in this relation, and is thus sensibly present to the mind, must necessarily be the object of these affections: there is as real a correspondence between them as between the lowest appetite of sense and its object.

That this Being is not a creature, but the Almighty God; that He is of infinite power and wisdom and goodness, does not render Him less the object of reverence and love than He would be if He had those attributes only in a limited degree. The Being who made us, and upon whom we entirely depend, is the object of some regards. He hath given us certain affections of mind, which correspond to wisdom, power, goodness, *i. e.* which are raised upon view of those qualities. If then He be really wise, powerful, good, He is the natural object of those affections which He hath endued us with, and which correspond to those attributes. That He is infinite in power, perfect in wisdom and goodness, makes no alteration, but only that He is the object of those affections raised to the highest pitch. He is not, indeed, to be discerned by any of our senses. *I go forward, but He is not there; and backward, but I cannot perceive Him: on the left hand where He doth work, but I cannot behold Him: He hideth Himself on the right hand, that I cannot see Him. Oh that I knew where I might find Him! that I might come even to His seat!* * But is He then afar off? does He not fill heaven and earth with His presence? The presence of our fellow-creatures affects our senses, and our senses give us the knowledge of their presence; which hath different kinds of influence upon us—love, joy, sorrow, restraint, encouragement, reverence. However, this influence is not immediately from our senses, but from that knowledge. Thus suppose a person neither to see nor hear another, not to know by any of his senses, but yet certainly to know, that another was with him; this knowledge might, and in many cases would, have one or more of the effects before mentioned. It is therefore not only reasonable, but also natural, to be affected with a presence, though it be not the object of our senses;

* Job xxii.

whether it be, or be not, is merely an accidental circumstance, which needs not come into consideration: it is the certainty that he is with us, and we with him, which hath the influence. We consider persons then as present, not only when they are within reach of our senses, but also when we are assured by any other means that they are within such a nearness; nay, if they are not, we can recall them to our mind, and be moved towards them as present; and must He, who is so much more intimately with us, that *in Him we live and move and have our being*, be thought too distant to be the object of our affections? We own and feel the force of amiable and worthy qualities in our fellow creatures; and can we be insensible to the contemplation of perfect goodness? Do we reverence the shadows of greatness here below, are we solicitous about honour and esteem and the opinion of the world, and shall we not feel the same with respect to Him whose are wisdom and power in the original, who *is the God of judgment by whom actions are weighed?* Thus love, reverence, desire of esteem, every faculty, every affection, tends towards and is employed about its respective object in common cases: and must the exercise of them be suspended with regard to Him alone who is an object, an infinitely more than adequate object, to our most exalted faculties; Him, *of whom, and through whom, and to whom are all things?*

As we cannot remove from this earth, or change our

general business on it, so neither can we alter our real nature. Therefore no exercise of the mind can be recommended, but only the exercise of those faculties you are conscious of. Religion does not demand new affections, but only claims the direction of those you already have, those affections you daily feel; though unhappily confined to objects not altogether unsuitable but altogether unequal to them. We only represent to you the higher, the adequate objects of those very faculties and affections. Let the man of ambition go on still to consider disgrace as the greatest evil, honour as his chief good. But disgrace in whose estimation? Honour in whose judgment? This is the only question. If shame, and delight in esteem, be spoken of as real, as any settled ground of pain or pleasure, both these must be in proportion to the supposed wisdom, and worth of him by whom we are contemned or esteemed. Must it then be thought enthusiastical to speak of a sensibility of this sort which shall have respect to an unerring judgment, to infinite wisdom, when we are assured this unerring judgment, this infinite wisdom does observe upon our actions?

It is the same with respect to the love of God in the strictest and most confined sense. We only offer and represent the highest object of an affection supposed already in your mind. Some degree of goodness must be previously supposed; this always implies the love of itself, an affection to goodness: the highest, the adequate object of this affection, is perfect goodness; which therefore we are to *love with all our heart, with all our soul, and with all our strength.* "Must we then, forgetting our own interest, as it were go out of ourselves, and love God for His own sake?" No more forget your own interest, no more go out of yourselves, than when you prefer one place, one prospect, the conversation of one man to that of another. Does not every affection necessarily imply that the object of it be itself loved? If it be not it is not the object of the affection. You may, and ought if you can, but it is a great mistake to think you can love or fear or hate anything, from consideration that such love or fear or hatred may be a means of obtaining good or avoiding evil. But the question whether we ought to love God for His sake or for our own being a mere mistake in language, the real question which this is mistaken for will, I suppose, be answered by observing that the goodness of God already exercised towards us, our present dependence upon Him, and our expectation of future benefits, ought, and have a natural tendency, to beget in us the affection of gratitude, and greater love towards Him, than the same goodness exercised towards others; were it only for this reason, that every affection is moved in proportion to the sense we have of the object of it; and we cannot but have a more lively sense of goodness when exercised towards ourselves than when exercised towards others. I added expectation of future benefits because the ground of that expectation is present goodness.

Thus Almighty God is the natural object of the several affections, love, reverence, fear, desire of approbation. For though He is simply one, yet we cannot but consider Him in partial and different views. He is in himself one uniform Being, and for ever the same without *variableness or shadow of turning;* but His infinite greatness, His goodness, His wisdom, are different objects to our mind. To which is to be added, that from the changes in our own characters, together with His unchangeableness, we cannot but consider ourselves as more or less the objects of His approbation, and really be so. For if He approves what is good, He cannot, merely from the unchangeableness of His nature, approve what is evil. Hence must arise more various movements of mind, more different kinds of affections. And this greater variety also is just and reasonable in such creatures as we are, though it respects a Being simply one, good and perfect. As some of these affections are most particularly suitable to so imperfect a creature as man in this mortal state we are passing through, so there may be other exercises of mind, or some of these in higher degrees, our employment and happiness in a state of perfection.

SERMON XIV.

Consider then our ignorance, the imperfection of our nature, our virtue, and our condition in this world, with respect to an infinitely good and just Being, our Creator and Governor, and you will see what religious affections of mind are most particularly suitable to this mortal state we are passing through.

Though we are not affected with anything so strongly as what we discern with our senses, and though our nature and condition require that we be much taken up about sensible things, yet our reason convinces us that God is present with us, and we see and feel the effects of His goodness: He is therefore the object of some regards. The imperfection of our virtue, joined with the consideration of His absolute rectitude or holiness, will scarce permit that perfection of love which entirely casts out all fear: yet goodness is the object of love to all creatures who have any degree of it themselves; and consciousness of a real endeavour to approve ourselves to Him, joined with the consideration of His goodness, as it quite excludes servile dread and horror, so it is plainly a reasonable ground for hope of His favour. Neither fear nor hope nor love then are excluded, and one or another of these will prevail, according to the different views we have of God, and ought to prevail, according to the changes we find in our own character. There is a temper of mind made up of, or which follows from all three, fear, hope, love—namely, resignation to the Divine will, which is the general temper belonging to this state; which ought to be the habitual frame of our mind and heart, and to be exercised at proper seasons more distinctly, in acts of devotion.

Resignation to the will of God is the whole of piety. It includes in it all that is good, and is a source of the most settled quiet and composure of mind. There is the general principle of submission in our nature. Man is not so constituted as to desire things, and be uneasy in the want of them, in proportion to their known value: many other considerations come in to determine the degrees of desire; particularly whether the advantage we take a view of be within the sphere of our rank. Whoever felt uneasiness upon observing any of the advantages brute creatures have over us? And yet it is plain they have several. It is the same with respect to advantages belonging to creatures of a superior order. Thus, though we see a thing to be highly valuable, yet that it does not belong to our condition of being is sufficient to suspend our desires after it, to make us rest satisfied without such advantage. Now there is just the same reason for quiet resignation in the want of everything equally unattainable. and out of our reach in particular, though others of our species be possessed of it. All this may be applied to the whole of life; to positive inconveniences as well as wants, not indeed to the sensations of pain and sorrow, but to all the uneasinesses of reflection, murmuring, and discontent. Thus is human nature formed to compliance, yielding, submission of temper. We find the principles of it within us; and every one exercises it towards some objects or other, *i.e.* feels it with regard to some persons and some circumstances. Now this is an excellent foundation of a reasonable and religious resignation. Nature teaches and inclines us to take up with our lot; the consideration that the course of things is unalterable hath a tendency to quiet the mind under it, to beget a submission of temper to it. But when we can add that this unalterable course is appointed and continued by infinite wisdom and goodness, how absolute should be our submission, how entire our trust and dependence!

This would reconcile us to our condition, prevent all the supernumerary troubles arising from imagination, distant fears, impatience—all uneasiness, except that which necessarily arises from the calamities themselves we may be under. How many of our cares should we by this means be disburdened of! Cares not properly our own, how apt soever they may be to intrude upon us, and we to admit them; the anxieties of expectation, solicitude about success and disappointment, which in truth are none of our concern. How open to every gratification would that mind be which was clear of these encumbrances!

Our resignation to the will of God may be said to be perfect when our will is lost and resolved up into His: when we rest in His will as our end, as being itself most just and right and good. And where is the impossibility of such an affection to what is just, and right, and good, such a loyalty of heart to the Governor of the universe as shall prevail over all sinister indirect desires of our own? Neither is this at bottom anything more than faith and honesty and fairness of mind—in a more enlarged sense indeed than those words are commonly used. And as, in common cases, fear and hope and other passions are raised in us by their respective objects, so this submission of heart and soul and mind, this religious resignation, would be as naturally produced by our having just conceptions of Almighty God, and a real sense of His presence with us. In how low a degree soever this temper usually prevails amongst men, yet it is a temper right in itself: it is what we owe to our Creator: it is particularly suitable to our mortal condition, and what we should endeavour after for our own sakes in our passage through such a world as this, where is nothing upon which we can rest or depend, nothing but what we are liable to be deceived and disappointed in. Thus we might *acquaint our-*

selves with God, and be at peace. This is piety and religion in the strictest sense, considered as a habit of mind: an habitual sense of God's presence with us; being affected towards Him, as present, in the manner His superior nature requires from such a creature as man: this is to *walk with God.*

Little more need be said of devotion or religious worship than that it is this temper exerted into act. The nature of it consists in the actual exercise of those affections towards God which are supposed habitual in good men. He is always equally present with us: but we are so much taken up with sensible things that, *Lo, He goeth by us, and we see Him not: He passeth on also, but we perceive Him not.** Devotion is retirement from the world He has made to Him alone: it is to withdraw from the avocations of sense, to employ our attention wholly upon Him, as upon an object actually present, to yield ourselves up to the influence of the Divine presence, and to give full scope to the affections of gratitude, love, reverence, trust, and dependence; of which infinite power, wisdom, and goodness is the natural and only adequate object. We may apply to the whole of devotion those words of the Son of Sirach, *When you glorify the Lord, exalt Him as much as you can; for even yet will He far exceed: and when you exalt Him, put forth all your strength, and be not weary; for you*

* Job ix. 2.

can never go far enough.* Our most raised affections of every kind cannot but fall short and be disproportionate when an infinite being is the object of them. This is the highest exercise and employment of mind that a creature is capable of. As this divine service and worship is itself absolutely due to God, so also is it necessary in order to a further end, to keep alive upon our minds a sense of His authority, a sense that in our ordinary behaviour amongst men we act under him as our Governor and Judge.

Thus you see the temper of mind respecting God which is particularly suitable to a state of imperfection, to creatures in a progress of being towards somewhat further.

Suppose now this something further attained, that we were arrived at it, what a perception will it be to see and know and feel that our trust was not vain, our dependence not groundless? That the issue, event, and consummation came out such as fully to justify and answer that resignation? If the obscure view of the divine perfection which we have in this world ought in just consequence to beget an entire resignation, what will this resignation be exalted into when *we shall see face to face, and know as we are known?* If we cannot form any distinct notion of that perfection of the love of God which *casts out all fear,* of that enjoyment of Him which will be

* Ecclus. xliii. 30.

the happiness of good men hereafter, the consideration of our wants and capacities of happiness, and that He will be an adequate supply to them, must serve us instead of such distinct conception of the particular happiness itself.

Let us then suppose a man entirely disengaged from business and pleasure, sitting down alone and at leisure, to reflect upon himself and his own condition of being. He would immediately feel that he was by no means complete of himself, but totally insufficient for his own happiness. One may venture to affirm that every man hath felt this, whether he hath again reflected upon it or not. It is feeling this deficiency, that they are unsatisfied with themselves, which makes men look out for assistance from abroad, and which has given rise to various kinds of amusements, altogether needless any otherwise than as they serve to fill up the blank spaces of time, and so hinder their feeling this deficiency, and being uneasy with themselves. Now, if these external things we take up with were really an adequate supply to this deficiency of human nature, if by their means our capacities and desires were all satisfied and filled up, then it might be truly said that we had found out the proper happiness of man, and so might sit down satisfied, and be at rest in the enjoyment of it. But if it appears that the amusements which men usually pass their time in are so far from coming up to or answering our notions and desires of happiness or good that they are really no more than what they are commonly called, somewhat to pass away the time, *i.e.* somewhat which serves to turn us aside from, and prevent our attending to, this our internal poverty and want; if they serve only, or chiefly, to suspend instead of satisfying our conceptions and desires of happiness; if the want remains, and we have found out little more than barely the means of making it less sensible; then are we still to seek for somewhat to be an adequate supply to it. It is plain that there is a capacity in the nature of man which neither riches nor honours nor sensual gratifications, nor anything in this world, can perfectly fill up or satisfy: there is a deeper and more essential want than any of these things can be the supply of. Yet surely there is a possibility of somewhat which may fill up all our capacities of happiness, somewhat in which our souls may find rest, somewhat which may be to us that satisfactory good we are inquiring after. But it cannot be anything which is valuable only as it tends to some further end. Those therefore who have got this world so much into their hearts as not to be able to consider happiness as consisting in anything but property and possessions—which are only valuable as the means to somewhat else—cannot have the least glimpse of the subject before us, which is the end, not the means; the thing itself, not somewhat in order to it. But if you can lay aside that general, confused, undeterminate notion of happiness, as consisting in such possessions, and fix in your thoughts that it really can consist in nothing but in a faculty's having its proper object, you will clearly see that in the coolest way of consideration, without either the heat of fanciful enthusiasm or the warmth of real devotion, nothing is more certain than that an infinite Being may Himself be, if He pleases, the supply to all the capacities of our nature. All the common enjoyments of life are from the faculties He hath endued us with and the objects He hath made suitable to them. He may Himself be to us infinitely more than all these; He may be to us all that we want. As our understanding can contemplate itself, and our affections be exercised upon themselves by reflection, so may each be employed in the same manner upon any other mind; and since the Supreme Mind, the Author and Cause of all things, is the highest possible object to Himself, He may be an adequate supply to all the faculties of our souls, a subject to our understanding, and an object to our affections.

Consider then: when we shall have put off this mortal body, when we shall be divested of sensual appetites, and those possessions which are now the means of gratification shall be of no avail, when this restless scene of business and vain pleasures, which now diverts us from ourselves, shall be all over, we, our proper self, shall still remain: we shall still continue the same creatures we are, with wants to be supplied and capacities of happiness. We must have faculties of perception, though not sensitive ones; and pleasure or uneasiness from our perceptions, as now we have.

There are certain ideas which we express by the words order, harmony, proportion, beauty, the furthest removed from anything sensual. Now what is there in those intellectual images, forms, or ideas, which begets that approbation, love, delight, and even rapture, which is seen in some persons' faces upon having those objects present to their minds?—"Mere enthusiasm!"—Be it what it will: there are objects, works of nature and of art, which all mankind have delight from quite distinct from their affording gratification to sensual appetites, and from quite another view of them than as being for their interest and further advantage. The faculties from which we are capable of these pleasures, and the pleasures themselves, are as natural, and as much to be accounted for, as any sensual appetite whatever, and the pleasure from its gratification. Words to be sure are wanting upon this subject; to say that everything of grace and beauty throughout the whole of nature, everything excellent and amiable shared in differently lower degrees by the whole creation, meet in the Author and Cause of all things, this is an inadequate and perhaps improper way of speaking of the Divine nature; but it is manifest that absolute rectitude, the perfection of being, must be in all senses, and in every respect, the highest object to the mind.

In this world it is only the effects of wisdom and power and greatness which we discern; it is not impossible that hereafter the qualities themselves in the supreme Being may be the immediate object of contemplation. What amazing wonders are opened to view by late improvements! What an object is the universe to a creature, if there be a creature who can comprehend its system! But it must be an infinitely higher exercise of the understanding to view the scheme of it in that mind which projected it before its foundations were laid. And surely we have meaning to the words when we speak of going further, and viewing, not only this system in His mind, but the wisdom and intelligence itself from whence it proceeded. The same may be said of power. But since wisdom and power are not God, He is a wise, a powerful Being; the divine nature may therefore be a further object to the understanding. It is nothing to observe that our senses give us but an imperfect knowledge of things: effects themselves, if we knew them thoroughly, would give us but imperfect notions of wisdom and power; much less of His being in whom they reside. I am not speaking of any fanciful notion of seeing all things in God, but only representing to you how much a higher object to the understanding an infinite Being Himself is than the things which He has made; and this is no more than saying that the Creator is superior to the works of His hands.

This may be illustrated by a low example. Suppose a machine, the sight of which would raise, and discoveries in its contrivance gratify, our curiosity: the real delight in this case would arise from its being the effect of skill and contrivance. This skill in the mind of the artificer would be a higher object, if we had any senses or ways to discern it. For, observe, the contemplation of that principle, faculty, or power which produced any effect must be a higher exercise of the understanding than the contemplation of the effect itself. The cause must be a higher object to the mind than the effect.

But whoever considers distinctly what the delight of knowledge is will see reason to be satisfied that it cannot be the chief good of man: all this, as it is applicable, so it was mentioned with regard to the attribute of goodness. I say goodness. Our being and all our enjoyments are the effects of it: just men bear its resemblance; but how little do we know of the orignal, of what it is in itself? Recall what was before observed concerning the affection to moral characters—which, in how low a degree soever, yet is plainly natural to man, and the most excellent part of his nature. Suppose this improved, as it may be improved, to any degree whatever, in the *spirits of just men made perfect*; and then suppose that they had a real view of that *righteousness which is an everlasting righteousness*, of the conformity of the Divine will to *the law of truth* in which the moral attributes of God consist, of that goodness in the sovereign Mind which gave birth to the universe. Add, what will be true of all good men hereafter, a consciousness of having an interest in what they are contemplating—suppose them able to say, *This God is our God for ever and ever.* Would they be any longer to seek for what was their chief happiness, their final good? Could the utmost stretch of their capacities look further? Would not infinite perfect goodness be their very end, the last end and object of their affections, beyond which they could neither have nor desire, beyond which they could not form a wish or thought?

Consider wherein that presence of a friend consists which has often so strong an effect as wholly to possess the mind, and entirely suspend all other affections and regards, and which itself affords the highest satisfaction and enjoyment. He is within reach of the senses. Now as our capacities of perception improve we shall have, perhaps by some faculty entirely new, a perception of God's presence with us in a nearer and stricter way, since it is certain He is more intimately present with us than anything else can be. Proof of the existence and presence of any being is quite different from the immediate perception, the consciousness of it. What then will be the joy of heart which His presence and *the light of His countenance*, who is the life of the universe, will inspire good men with when they shall have a sensation that He is the sustainer of their being, that they exist in Him; when they shall feel His influence to cheer and enliven and support their frame, in a manner of which we have now no conception? He will be in a literal sense *their strength and their portion for ever.*

When we speak of things so much above our comprehension as the employment and happiness of a future state, doubtless it behoves us to speak with all modesty and distrust of ourselves. But the Scripture represents the happiness of that state under the notions of *seeing God, seeing Him as He is, knowing as we are known, and seeing face to face.* These words are not general or undetermined, but express a particular determinate happiness. And I will be bold to say that nothing can account for or come up to those expressions but only this, that God Himself will be an object to our faculties, that He Himself will be our happiness as distinguished from the enjoyments of the present state, which seem to arise not immediately from Him but from the objects He has adapted to give us delight.

To conclude: Let us suppose a person tired with care and sorrow and the repetition of vain delights which fill up the round of life; sensible that everything here below in its best estate is altogether vanity. Suppose him to feel that deficiency of human nature before taken notice of, and to be convinced that God alone was the adequate supply to it. What could be more applicable to a good man in this state of mind, or better express his present wants and distant hopes, his passage through this world as a progress towards a state of perfection, than the following passages in the devotions of the royal prophet? They are plainly in a higher and more proper sense applicable to this than they could be to anything else. *I have seen an end of all perfection. Whom have I in heaven but Thee? And there is none upon earth that I desire in comparison of Thee. My flesh and my heart faileth: but God is the strength of my heart and my portion for ever. Like as the hart desireth the water-brooks, so longeth my soul after Thee, O God. My soul is athirst for God, yea, even for the living God: when shall I come to appear before Him? How excellent is Thy lovingkindness, O God! and the children of men shall put their trust under the shadow of Thy wings. They shall be satisfied with the plenteousness of Thy house: and Thou shalt give them drink of Thy pleasures, as out of the river. For with Thee is the well of life: and in Thy light shall we see light. Blessed is the man whom Thou choosest, and receivest unto Thee: he shall dwell in Thy court, and shall be satisfied with the pleasures of Thy house, even of Thy holy temple. Blessed is the people,*

O Lord, that can rejoice in Thee: they shall walk in the light of Thy countenance. Their delight shall be daily in Thy name, and in Thy righteousness shall they make their boast. For Thou art the glory of their strength: and in Thy lovingkindness they shall be exalted. As for me, I will behold Thy presence in righteousness: and when I awake up after Thy likeness, I shall be satisfied with it. Thou shalt shew me the path of life; in Thy presence is the fulness of joy, and at Thy right hand there is pleasure for evermore.

www.ingramcontent.com/pod-product-compliance
Lightning Source LLC
Chambersburg PA
CBHW020846160426
43192CB00007B/806